Easy

Fast. Fashionable. Fun.

Beading

Vol. 4

The best projects from the fourth year of *BeadStyle* magazine

KALMBACH
BOOKS

12 11 10 09 08   1 2 3 4 5

**The designs in this book are for your personal use.
They are not intended for resale.**

All projects have appeared previously in
BeadStyle magazine.

Printed in China

Visit our Web site at
BeadAndCraftBooks.com
Secure online ordering available

Publisher's Cataloging-In-Publication Data
(Prepared by The Donohue Group, Inc.)

Easy beading. Vol. 4 : fast, fashionable, fun : the best projects from
   the fourth year of BeadStyle magazine.

   p., : col. ill. ; cm.
   All projects have appeared previously in BeadStyle magazine.
   Includes index.
   ISBN: 978-0-87116-263-2

1. Beadwork--Handbooks, manuals, etc. 2. Beads--Handbooks,
manuals, etc. 3. Jewelry making--Handbooks, manuals, etc. I.
Title: BeadStyle Magazine.

TT860 .E27 2008
745.594/2

Contents

**On the cover
Page 214**

String a bold pendant

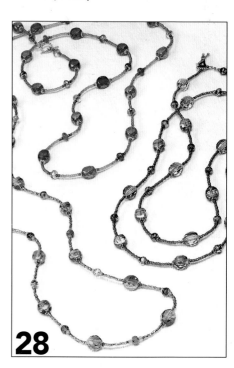

28

Glass and ceramic

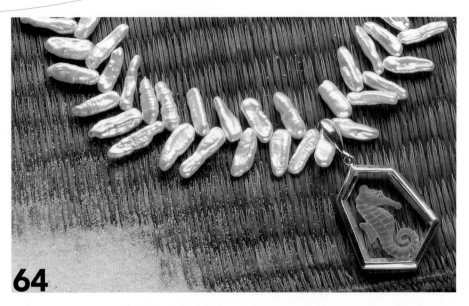

64

Pearls and shells

100

133

188

Crystals

190

Mixed materials

Look for great shortcuts on these pages:
41, 81, 119, 163, 197, 253

Introduction

I love to look over the *Easy Beading* books. This is our fourth volume, and each time I'm asked to look at the proofs, I browse the pages with a mix of nostalgia and appreciation. Sometimes when we're putting together the individual issues, things get too busy to really sit back and appreciate the beauty of the individual projects. Also, when I see all the projects together, the variety and range of styles is pretty impressive. I shouldn't be surprised, though. *BeadStyle* is blessed with an incredible group of contributors. Their backgrounds and tastes are very different. They each have their own story and they share a bit of it in every piece of jewelry they make for us. We get jewelry from around the globe and from down the hallway. If you like a particular project, I urge you to make a new friend and e-mail the designer. Contact information for our contributors is on page 254. I encourage you to turn the pages and meet Rupa Balachandar (p. 106), Jean Yates (p. 239), Brenda Schweder (p. 51), and Steven James (p. 90). They're just some of the more than 50 artists represented in these pages. Want to get together more than once a year? We do, too! Check out *BeadStyle* magazine on your favorite newsstand or subscribe at beadstylemag.com.

As in previous volumes, we've organized this fourth volume of *Easy Beading* by materials used: Glass and ceramic, Pearls and shells, Metal and chain, Gemstones, Crystals, and Mixed materials. You'll notice that within each material category, there's a whole world to explore. Mixed materials are very different things to Julie Paasch-Anderson (p. 201) and Roxie Moede (p. 234).

There are projects for any skill level or attention span. We know that while your style and creativity are limitless, your time is not. You can make any of these projects in a couple of hours tops. Now deciding what to do first — that will take some time. So get to it! I hope you enjoy them as much as we did.

Warmest regards,

Cathy

Cathryn Jakicic
Editor, *BeadStyle* magazine

Beader's glossary

A visual guide to gemstones, beads, findings, and tools

gemstone shapes

lentil

rondelle

button or rondelle

round

oval

marquise

rectangle

tube

briolette

drop

chips

nugget

crystal and glass

Czech fire-polished

bicone

cube

oval

drop

briolette

cone

round crystal

saucer

top-drilled saucer (with jump ring)

flat back

flat back

rhinestone squaredelle

dichroic

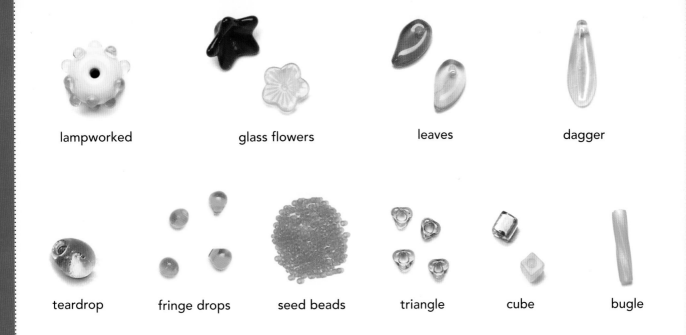

lampworked   glass flowers   leaves   dagger

teardrop   fringe drops   seed beads   triangle   cube   bugle

pearls, shells, and miscellaneous

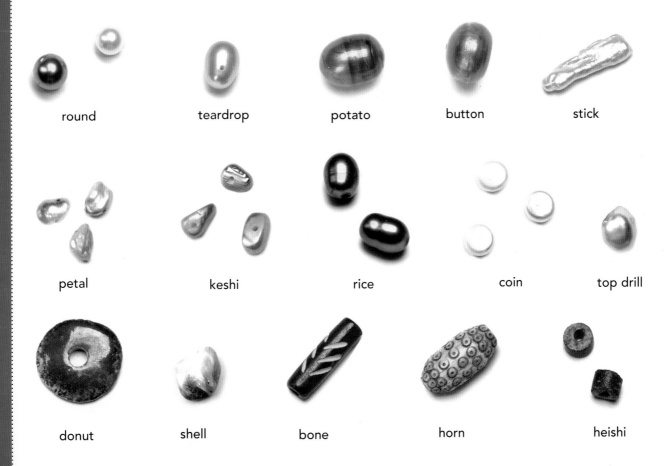

round   teardrop   potato   button   stick

petal   keshi   rice   coin   top drill

donut   shell   bone   horn   heishi

findings, spacers, and connectors

French hook
ear wires

post earring
finding

hoop earring

lever-back
earring finding

earring
threader

magnetic
clasp

S-hook
clasp

lobster claw
clasp

toggle
clasp

two-strand
toggle clasp

box clasp

slide clasp

hook-and-eye
clasps

snap clasp

pinch crimp
end

crimp ends

coil end

tube-shaped and
round crimp beads

crimp
covers

bead tips

jump rings and
soldered jump rings

split ring

spacers

bead caps

filigree
stamping

multistrand
spacer bars

two-strand
curved tube

single-strand
tube

three-to-one and two-
to-one connectors

bail

cone

tools, stringing materials, and chain

crimping pliers

chainnose pliers

roundnose pliers

bentnose pliers

split-ring pliers

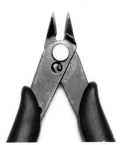
diagonal wire cutters

heavy-duty wire cutters

ring mandrel

twisted wire beading needle

decorative head pin, head pin, eye pin

sterling silver wire

memory wire

colored craft wire

leather cord

suede cord

waxed linen

beading thread/cord

flexible beading wire

curb chain

rolo chain

long-and-short chain

figaro chain

cable chain

Basics

A step-by-step reference to key jewelry-making techniques used in bead-stringing projects.

plain loop

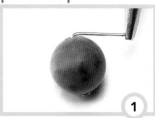

1

Trim the wire or head pin ⅜ in. (1cm) above the top bead. Make a right angle bend close to the bead.

2

Grab the wire's tip with round-nose pliers. The tip of the wire should be flush with the pliers. Roll the wire to form a half circle. Release the wire.

3

Reposition the pliers in the loop and continue rolling.

4

The finished loop should form a centered circle above the bead.

wrapped loop

1

Make sure you have at least 1¼ in. (3.2cm) of wire above the bead. With the tip of your chainnose pliers, grasp the wire directly above the bead. Bend the wire (above the pliers) into a right angle.

2

Using roundnose pliers, position the jaws in the bend as shown.

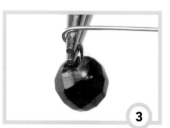

3

Bring the wire over the top jaw of the roundnose pliers.

4

Reposition the pliers' lower jaw snugly into the loop. Curve the wire downward around the bottom of the roundnose pliers. This is the first half of a wrapped loop.

5

Position the chainnose pliers' jaws across the loop.

6

Wrap the wire around the wire stem, covering the stem between the loop and the top bead. Trim the excess wire and press the cut end close to the wraps with chainnose pliers.

opening and closing loops or jump rings

1

Hold the loop or jump ring with two pairs of chainnose pliers or chainnose and roundnose pliers, as shown.

2

To open the loop or jump ring, bring one pair of pliers toward you and push the other pair away. Reverse the steps to close the open loop or jump ring.

split ring

To open a split ring, slide the hooked tip of split-ring pliers between the two overlapping wires.

surgeon's knot

Cross the right end over the left end and go through the loop. Go through again. Pull the ends to tighten. Cross the left end over the right end and go through once. Pull the ends to tighten.

overhand knot

Make a loop and pass the working end through it. Pull the ends to tighten the knot.

lark's head knot

Fold a cord in half and lay it behind a ring, loop, etc. with the fold pointing down. Bring the ends through the ring from back to front, then through the fold and tighten.

making wraps above a top-drilled bead

1

Center a top-drilled bead on a 3-in. (7.6cm) piece of wire. Bend each wire upward to form a squared-off U shape.

2

Cross the wires into an X above the bead.

3

Using chainnose pliers, make a small bend in each wire so the ends form a right angle.

4

Wrap the horizontal wire around the vertical wire as in a wrapped loop. Trim the excess wrapping wire.

folded crimp end

1

Glue one end of the cord and place it in a crimp end. Use chainnose pliers to fold one side of the crimp end over the cord.

2

Repeat on the second side and squeeze gently. Test to be sure the crimp end is secure.

flattened crimp

1

Hold the crimp using the tip of your chainnose pliers. Squeeze the pliers firmly to flatten the crimp.

2

Tug the wire to make sure the crimp has a solid grip. If the wire slides, repeat the steps with a new crimp.

folded crimp

1

Position the crimp bead in the notch closest to the crimping pliers' handle.

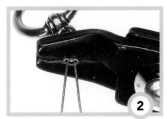

2

Separate the wires and firmly squeeze the crimp.

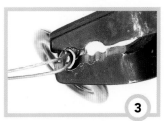

3

Move the crimp into the notch at the pliers' tip and hold the crimp as shown. Squeeze the crimp bead, folding it in half at the indentation.

4

Test that the folded crimp is secure.

cutting flexible beading wire

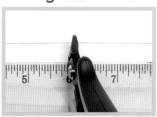

Decide how long you want your necklace to be. Add 6 in. (15cm) and cut a piece of beading wire to that length. (For a bracelet, add 5 in./13cm.)

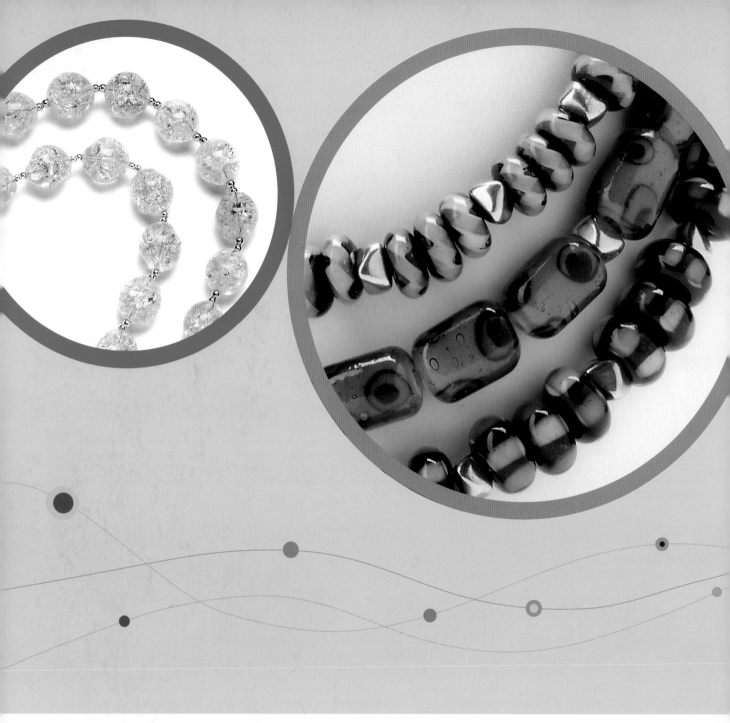

Glass and

ceramic

Take a shine

Showcase enamel components in a necklace, bracelet, and earrings

by Christianne Camera

These projects show you three ways to turn enameled copper components into jewelry. Crystals and seed beads form a simple pendant necklace, while wrapped loops link components in a contemporary bracelet. For the easiest drop earrings, just turn plain loops. Whatever the method, your results will shine.

1 **necklace** • Open a jump ring (Basics, p. 12). Attach a pendant and close the jump ring.

2 Determine the finished length of your necklace. (The pink necklace is 16 in./41cm; the brown necklace, 18½ in./47cm.) Add 6 in. (15cm) and cut a piece of beading wire to that length. Center the pendant and an 11º seed bead on the wire.

3 On each end, string: crystal, 11º, 10º, 11º, 10º, 11º. Repeat until the strand is within 1 in. (2.5cm) of the desired length.

4 On each end, string a crimp bead, an 11º, and half of a clasp. Go back through the last few beads strung, and tighten the wire. Check the fit, and add or remove beads from each end if necessary. Crimp the crimp beads (Basics) and trim the excess wire.

to enamel

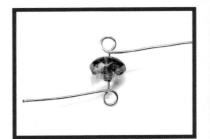

1 **bracelet** • Cut a 3-in. (7.6cm) piece of wire. Using the largest part of your roundnose pliers, make the first half of a wrapped loop (Basics, p. 12). String a crystal and make the first half of a wrapped loop.

2 Attach one hole of an enamel component to each loop, and complete the wraps.

3 Continue attaching crystal units and components until the bracelet is within 1 in. (2.5cm) of the desired length. End with a crystal unit, leaving the end loops unwrapped.

4 On each end loop, attach half of the clasp. Complete the wraps.

1 **earrings** • Cut a 1-in. (2.5cm) piece of wire. Make a plain loop (Basics, p. 12). String a crystal and an 11º seed bead. Make a plain loop perpendicular to the bottom loop.

2 Open the bottom loop (Basics) and attach an enamel component. Close the loop.

Open the loop of an earring wire and attach the dangle. Close the loop. Make a second earring to match the first. ❖

Supply List

necklace
- 32mm round enamel pendant (C-Koop Beads, 218-525-7333, ckoopbeads@yahoo.com)
- **28–40** 6mm crystals
- 2g 10º twisted hex-cut beads
- 2g 11º seed beads
- flexible beading wire, .014 or .015
- 6mm inside diameter jump ring
- **2** crimp beads
- toggle clasp
- chainnose and roundnose pliers, or **2** pairs of chainnose pliers
- diagonal wire cutters
- crimping pliers (optional)

bracelet
- **4–5** 18 x 25mm oval two-hole enamel components (C-Koop Beads)
- **5–6** 6mm crystals
- 15–18 in. (38–46cm) 22- or 24-gauge half-hard wire
- toggle clasp
- chainnose and roundnose pliers
- diagonal wire cutters

earrings
- **2** 15mm round enamel components (C-Koop Beads)
- **2** 6mm crystals
- **2** 11º seed beads
- 2 in. (5cm) 24-gauge half-hard wire
- pair of earring wires
- chainnose and roundnose pliers
- diagonal wire cutters

String a
BEADED
BOUQUET

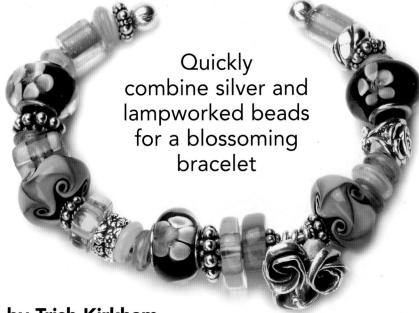

Quickly
combine silver and
lampworked beads
for a blossoming
bracelet

by Trish Kirkham

Arrange your bouquet with lampworked beads and
off-center flower charms. Preserve your wrist corsage
by gluing the bead ends, or skip the adhesive and
change beads with the seasons.

Supply List

- cuff bracelet with twist-off bead ends (Fire Mountain Gems, 800-355-2137, firemountaingems.com)
- 5–9 14–20mm lampworked beads (blue/purple lampworked beads by Motavenda Melchizedek, innerworlddesigns.com; green/black swirl beads by Jeff Plath, available from Eclectica, 262-641-0910)
- 5–15 8–12mm large-hole glass beads
- 3 10–12mm charms with attached loop
- 15–30 6–12mm large-hole spacers
- G-S Hypo Cement (optional)

1 Unscrew one bead end of a cuff bracelet. String beads and spacers over one-third of the bracelet's length.

2 String three charms. String beads and spacers over the remaining length of the bracelet.

3 Reattach the bead end. If desired, apply adhesive to the threads of the bead ends prior to attaching. ❧

Pre-Columbian ART

String a traditional-style necklace with soothing ceramic beads

by Cathy Jakicic

The Colombian Craft Connection was created to foster economic growth for Colombia's youth, women, and indigenous peoples. Pre-Columbian art is characterized by angular, linear patterns and three-dimensional ceramics. The company's Pre-Columbian-style clay beads are made with mixtures of earthenware clays, silica, and other minerals — all nontoxic materials. They are colored with various proportions of oxides and then fired. For more information, call (713) 995-8469 or visit colombiancraftconnection .com.

1 Decide how long you want your necklace to be. (My strands are 22 in., 24½ in., and 25½ in./56cm, 62.2cm, and 64.8cm.)

For the shortest strand: Unwind a card of beading cord. Tie an overhand knot (Basics, p. 12) 6 in. (15cm) from the end of the cord without the needle. String a 5mm heishi bead, a tube bead, and a 5mm heishi. Tie an overhand knot next to the last bead. Repeat the pattern, leaving 1–1½ in. (2.5–3.8cm) between each bead segment, until the strand is within 6–7 in. (15–18cm) of the finished length.

2 For the middle strand, follow step 1, changing the bead sequence to: 3mm heishi, tube, 3mm heishi, tube, 3mm heishi, tube, 3mm heishi. Leave ½ in. (1.3cm) between each bead segment.

3 For the longest strand, follow step 1, changing the bead sequence to: 3mm heishi, 7mm heishi, 3mm heishi. Leave 1–1½ in. (2.5–3.8cm) between each bead segment.

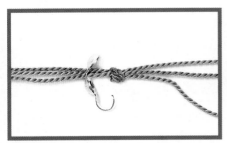

4 String one end of each strand through a bead tip. Check the fit, allowing 1 in. (2.5cm) for the clasp. Make an overhand knot with all three strands 2–3 in. (5–7.6cm) from the end bead, adjusting the strands as desired. Repeat on the other side.

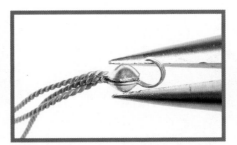

5 Trim the excess cord and apply glue to each knot. Close the bead tips over the knots using chainnose pliers.

6 On each end, attach half of the clasp to the loop of the bead tip. Close the loop. ✤

SupplyList

- **50–56** 5–10mm tube beads
- **14–20** 7mm heishi beads
- **22–26** 5mm heishi beads
- **80–92** 3mm heishi beads
- **3** cards of nylon beading cord with attached needle, size 4 or 5
- **2** bead tips
- toggle clasp
- chainnose pliers
- G-S Hypo Cement

EDITOR'S TIPS
- Stringing the non-needle end of the cords through the bead tip is easier if you use a twisted-wire beading needle.
- Use a flat iron to quickly remove any kinks in the nylon cord.

Explore the many
options of a
monochromatic
palette

by **Lisa Belden**

Monochromatic doesn't mean dull.
Use a variety of beads in different shades of
one dominant hue to make a chunky
bracelet. Beads of different sizes and shapes
make for a richly textured piece. Look to
your wardrobe for a prominent color, or
make a collection of bracelets, each featuring
shades within one color family.

Keep your
COLORS
all in the family

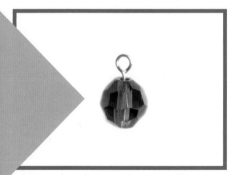

1 On a head pin, string a 4–12mm bead. Make a plain loop (Basics, p. 12). Make 35 to 40 bead units.

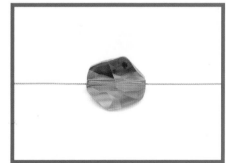

2 Cut a piece of beading wire (Basics). Center a focal bead on the wire.

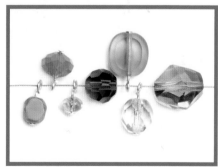

3 On each end, string three bead units, a 4–12mm bead, two bead units, and a 4–12mm bead. Repeat until the strand is within 2 in. (5cm) of the finished length. End with a 4–12mm bead.

EDITOR'S TIP
For each bead unit, be sure to close the plain loop tightly so it won't slip off the beading wire.

23

4 On one end, string a crimp bead, a bicone crystal, and a soldered jump ring. Repeat on the other end, substituting a clasp for the soldered jump ring. Check the fit, and add or remove beads if necessary. On each end, go back through the beads just strung and tighten the wire. Crimp the crimp bead (Basics) and trim the excess wire.

5 Cut a 2-in. (5cm) piece of 20-gauge wire. Make the first half of a wrapped loop (Basics). String a 4–12mm bead and make the first half of a wrapped loop. Repeat to make a second bead unit.

6 On a head pin, string a 4–12mm bead. Make the first half of a wrapped loop.

7 Attach the bead units as shown. Complete the wraps, leaving the top loop unwrapped.

8 Attach the dangle to the soldered jump ring. Complete the wraps. ✤

SupplyList

- 14–16mm focal bead
- **45–55** 4–12mm beads, in assorted shapes
- **2** 4mm bicone crystals
- flexible beading wire, .014 or .015
- 4 in. (10cm) 20-gauge half-hard wire
- **36–41** 1½-in. (3.8cm) 22-gauge head pins
- 4mm soldered jump ring
- **2** crimp beads
- spring-ring clasp
- chainnose and roundnose pliers
- diagonal wire cutters
- crimping pliers (optional)

String a
crackle-glass
necklace in a snap

Beads and chain make an airy combination

by Karen Burdette

For a quick project with plenty of flash, string a short strand of crackle-glass beads and finish it with chain. The beads' tiny fractures make this easy design pop.

SupplyList

- **15–17** 16mm crackle-glass beads (Michaels, michaels.com for store locations)
- **32–36** 3–4mm round spacers
- flexible beading wire, .014 or .015
- **4–8** in. (10–20cm) chain, 4–6mm links
- **2** 4–5mm jump rings
- **2** crimp beads
- toggle clasp
- chainnose and roundnose pliers
- diagonal wire cutters
- crimping pliers (optional)

DESIGN OPTION
Try replacing the spacers with accent beads that match the color of the crackle glass. If you like, start the necklace by centering an accent bead on the wire.

1 Cut an 18-in. (46cm) piece of beading wire. On the wire, center two spacers, a 16mm bead, and two spacers.

2 On each end, string a 16mm and two spacers. Repeat six or seven times. End with a 16mm.

3 Decide how long you want your necklace to be. (My necklaces are 17 in./43cm.) Subtract 12 in. (30cm), and cut a piece of chain to that length. Cut the chain in half.

On each end of the beaded strand, string a spacer, a crimp bead, a spacer, and a chain. Go back through the last few beads strung and tighten the wire. Crimp the crimp bead (Basics, p. 12) and trim the excess wire.

4 Check the fit, and trim chain from each end if necessary. On each end, open a jump ring (Basics) and attach the chain and half of a clasp. Close the jump ring. ❖

Swayed by suede

Wire an art glass
bead in place for
a quick bracelet

by Paulette Biedenbender

This suede bracelet provides a casual setting for your favorite art bead. With a variety of beads and cords available, you can quickly create a stylish color combination custom-made for your wardrobe.

1 Determine the finished length of your bracelet and double that measurement. Subtract 1 in. (2.5cm) and cut a piece of suede cord to that length.
Center a bead cap, an art bead, and a bead cap on the cord.

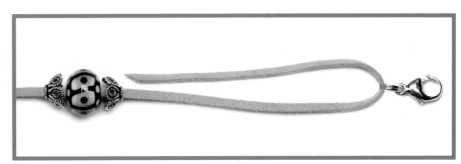

2 On one end, string a lobster claw clasp. If the clasp's loop is not large enough to accommodate the cord, attach a split ring to the clasp. Fold the cord in half.

3 Cut a 6-in. (15cm) piece of wire and gently fold it in half. Place the fold of the wire ¼ in. (6mm) from the bead cap. Wrap each end of the wire around the cord, using chainnose pliers to prevent the wire from slipping.

4 Using chainnose pliers, flatten the finished wraps. Repeat steps 2 and 3 on the other end, omitting the clasp. ❖

EDITOR'S TIP
For even, horizontal wraps, wrap the wire on one side of the cord, then flip the bracelet over to wrap the other side of the cord. Repeat until wrapping is complete.

Supply List

- 12–20mm large-hole art bead (Glass Onion Studios, 920-733-2853, glassonion.biz)
- 2 10–12mm large-hole bead caps
- 12 in. (30cm) 22-gauge, half-round, half-hard wire
- lobster claw clasp
- 6mm split ring (optional)
- 12–14 in. (30–36cm) 3mm suede cord
- chainnose pliers
- diagonal wire cutters
- split-ring pliers (optional)

LONG& LUSTROUS

Glass beads and seed beads make a necklace sparkle

by Maria Camera

String a long, versatile necklace economically with seed beads and faceted glass beads. Because the necklace has a clasp, you'll have the option to wear it wrapped twice. This necklace also looks gorgeous layered with lengthy gold chains.

1 necklace • Cut a piece of beading wire (Basics, p. 12). (My necklaces are 38 in./.97m.) Center: color B 11º seed bead, spacer, 10mm bead, spacer, color B 11º.

2 On each end, string: ten color A 11ºs, color B 11º, 8º seed bead, rondelle, 8º, color B 11º, ten color A 11ºs, color B 11º, spacer, 10mm bead, spacer, color B 11º. Repeat until the strand is within 1 in. (2.5cm) of the finished length.

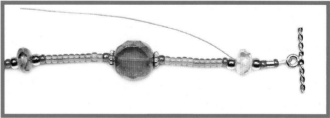

3 On each end, string a color B 11º, a crimp bead, a color B 11º, and half of the clasp. Check the fit, and add or remove beads from each end if necessary. Tighten the wire and crimp the crimp bead (Basics). Trim the excess wire.

> **EDITOR'S TIP**
> Double-check that the pattern is correct as you string your necklace. It's easier than removing beads later to fix a mistake.

1 **earrings** • On a decorative head pin, string a 10mm bead, two spacers, an 8º seed bead, and three 11º seed beads. Make a wrapped loop (Basics, p. 12).

2 Open an earring wire (Basics). Attach the dangle and close the wire. Make a second earring to match the first. ❖

Supply List

necklace
- **17–21** 10mm faceted glass beads
- **18–22** 5–6mm rondelles
- 2g 8º seed beads
- 5g 11º seed beads, 4g in color A, 1g in color B
- **34–42** 4mm spacers
- flexible beading wire, .014 or .015
- **2** crimp beads
- toggle clasp
- chainnose or crimping pliers
- diagonal wire cutters

earrings
- **2** 10mm faceted glass beads
- **2** 8º seed beads
- **6** 11º seed beads
- **4** 4mm spacers
- **2** 2-in. (5cm) decorative head pins
- pair of earring wires
- chainnose and roundnose pliers
- diagonal wire cutters

Embrace the exotic

Conjure up a
colorful travel
fantasy with a
kashmiri-bead
necklace and
bracelet

by Deborah Lacher

Kashmiri beads are traditional Indian beads formed from clay resin and then decorated with glass, sequins, ceramic, and brass. Combine these fancy beads with shapely gemstones for a vibrant necklace and bracelet.

1 necklace • Cut a piece of beading wire (Basics, p. 12). (My necklaces are 17 in./43cm.) String: 5mm spacer, 9mm round bead, 7mm spacer, kashmiri bead, 7mm spacer, 9mm round, 5mm spacer. Center the beads on the wire.

2 On each end, string: nugget, flat bead, top-drilled bead, 5mm spacer, kashmiri bead, 5mm spacer, barrel-shaped bead.

3 On each end, string: flat bead, 7mm spacer, nugget, 7mm spacer, flat bead, 5mm spacer, nugget, 5mm spacer, flat bead.

4 On each end, string: 5mm spacer, barrel, 5mm spacer, barrel, flat bead, barrel. Repeat until the strand is within 2 in. (5cm) of the desired length.

5 On one end, string a round spacer, a crimp bead, a round spacer, and a lobster claw clasp. Repeat on the other end, substituting a soldered jump ring for the clasp. Check the fit, and add or remove beads from each end if necessary. Go back through the last few beads strung and tighten the wire. Crimp the crimp beads (Basics) and trim the excess wire.

SupplyList

necklace
- **3** 20mm kashmiri beads (Spacetrader Beads, spacetrader.com.au)
- **6** gemstone nuggets, approximately 20mm
- **8–12** 12mm barrel-shaped beads
- **2** 10–12mm beads, top drilled
- **2** 9mm round beads
- **10–14** 7mm flat metal beads
- **6** 7mm spacers
- **14–18** 5mm spacers
- **4** 4mm round spacers
- flexible beading wire, .018 or .019
- **2** crimp beads
- lobster claw clasp and soldered jump ring
- chainnose or crimping pliers
- diagonal wire cutters

bracelet
- 20mm kashmiri bead (Spacetrader Beads, spacetrader.com.au)
- **2** gemstone nuggets, approximately 20mm
- **4–6** 12mm barrel-shaped beads
- **4** 7mm flat metal beads
- **2** 7mm spacers
- **4–6** 5mm spacers
- **4** 4mm round spacers
- flexible beading wire, .018 or .019
- **2** crimp beads
- toggle clasp
- chainnose or crimping pliers
- diagonal wire cutters

DESIGN OPTION
To complement the embellishments of your kashmiri beads, substitute flat gemstones for traditional metal spacers.

1 bracelet • Cut a piece of beading wire (Basics, p. 12). String: nugget, 7mm spacer, kashmiri bead, 7mm spacer, nugget. Center the beads on the wire.

2 On each end, string: flat bead, barrel-shaped bead, 5mm spacer, barrel, 5mm spacer. Repeat until the strand is within 2 in. (5cm) of the desired length.

3 On each end, string a round spacer, a crimp bead, a round spacer, and half of a clasp. Check the fit, and add or remove beads from each end if necessary. Go back through the last few beads strung and tighten the wire. Crimp the crimp bead (Basics) and trim the excess wire. ❖

Lampwork beads shine in this bold collar

Venetian-style beads from Indonesia

by Jane Konkel

On the island of Java, master bead maker Samodra and a team of 20 make lampworked beads. They use traditional gasoline-fueled torches called *minyak tanah* and locally made and imported glass rods. Spacetrader (spacetrader. com.au) is the international distributor of these lovely beads. A currency converter on their Web site will help you determine the price of the beads as well as shipping costs.

SupplyList

Venetian-style lampworked beads and chain from Spacetrader, spacetrader.com.au.

necklace
- 9-in. (23cm) strand 13mm lampworked barrel beads
- 9-in. (23cm) strand 11mm lampworked rondelles
- 9-in. (23cm) strand 9mm lampworked rondelles
- **26–32** 6mm spacers
- **6** 5mm spacers
- flexible beading wire, .014 or .015

- 10–12 in. (25–30cm) chain, 5–7mm links
- 5mm jump ring
- **6** crimp beads
- **6** crimp covers (optional)
- lobster claw clasp
- chainnose or crimping pliers
- diagonal wire cutters

earrings
- **2** 9mm lampworked rondelles
- **2** 5mm spacers
- 1½ in. (3.8cm) chain, 5–7mm links
- **2** 1½-in. (3.8cm) decorative head pins
- pair of earring wires
- chainnose and roundnose pliers
- diagonal wire cutters

1 necklace • Decide how long you want the beaded sections to be. (My beaded sections are 6½, 7½, and 8½ in./16.5, 19.1, and 21.6cm.) Add 6 in. (15cm) and cut a piece of beading wire to each length. On the shortest wire, string three 9mm rondelles and a 6mm spacer. Repeat until the strand is within 1 in. (2.5cm) of the desired length, ending with three rondelles.

2 On the middle wire, string three barrel beads and a 6mm spacer. Repeat until the strand is within 1 in. (2.5cm) of the desired length, ending with three barrels.

3 On the longest wire, string three 11mm rondelles and a 6mm spacer. Repeat until the strand is within 1 in. (2.5cm) of the desired length, ending with three rondelles.

4 Decide how long you want the chain section to be. (My chain section is 11 in./ 28cm.) Cut a piece of chain to that length, then cut the chain in half. On each end of each beaded strand, string a 6mm spacer, a crimp bead, a 5mm spacer, and one chain. Go back through the last few beads strung and tighten the wire. Crimp the crimp bead (Basics, p. 12) and trim the excess wire. If desired, close a crimp cover over each crimp.

5 Check the fit. Trim chain from each end, if necessary. Open a 5mm jump ring (Basics). Attach one chain end and a lobster claw clasp, and close the jump ring.

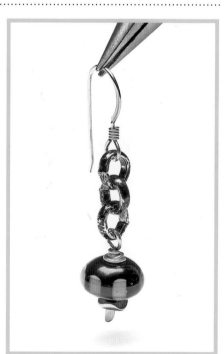

1 earrings • On a decorative head pin, string a spacer and a rondelle. Make the first half of a wrapped loop (Basics, p. 12).

2 Cut a ½-in. (1.3cm) piece of chain. Attach the bead unit and complete the wraps.

3 Open the loop of an earring wire (Basics). Attach the dangle and close the loop. Make a second earring to match the first. ❖

Simply endless possibilities

Intersperse translucent lampworked button beads with bright drops for a color-saturated bracelet

by Maria Camera

The simplicity of this bracelet's construction leaves room for limitless creativity with materials, plus time to put together a pair of earrings. Whether you stick with glass beads or mix in some pearls or metal spacers, simple will never be boring.

1 bracelet • Cut a piece of beading wire (Basics, p. 12). String an alternating pattern of button beads and teardrop-shaped beads until the strand is within 1 in. (2.5cm) of the desired length. End with a teardrop.

2 On each end, string an 11º seed bead, a crimp bead, an 11º, and half of a clasp. Check the fit, and add or remove beads if necessary. Go back through the last few beads strung and tighten the wire. Crimp the crimp bead (Basics) and trim the excess wire.

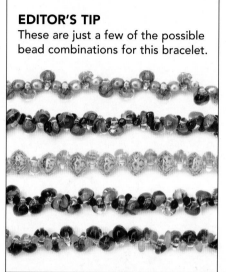

EDITOR'S TIP
These are just a few of the possible bead combinations for this bracelet.

SupplyList

bracelet
- **20–30** 10mm lampworked button beads (Eclectica, 262-641-0910)
- **21–31** 6 x 4mm glass teardrop-shaped beads
- **4** 11º seed beads
- flexible beading wire, .014 or .015
- **2** crimp beads
- toggle clasp
- chainnose or crimping pliers
- diagonal wire cutters

earrings
- **2** 10mm lampworked button beads (Eclectica, 262-641-0910)
- **2** 6 x 4mm glass teardrop-shaped beads
- **2** 8mm jump rings
- pair of earring wires
- chainnose and roundnose pliers or **2** pairs of chainnose pliers

1 earrings • Open an 8mm jump ring (Basics, p. 12). String a button bead and a teardrop-shaped bead.

2 Attach the dangle to the loop of an earring wire. Close the jump ring. Make a second earring to match the first. ❖

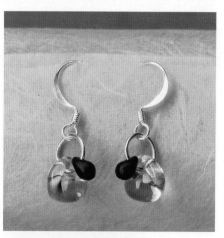

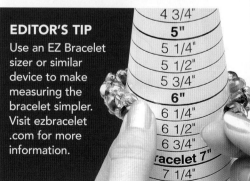

EDITOR'S TIP
Use an EZ Bracelet sizer or similar device to make measuring the bracelet simpler. Visit ezbracelet .com for more information.

4 3/4"
5"
5 1/4"
5 1/2"
5 3/4"
6"
6 1/4"
6 1/2"
6 3/4"
racelet 7"
7 1/4"

37

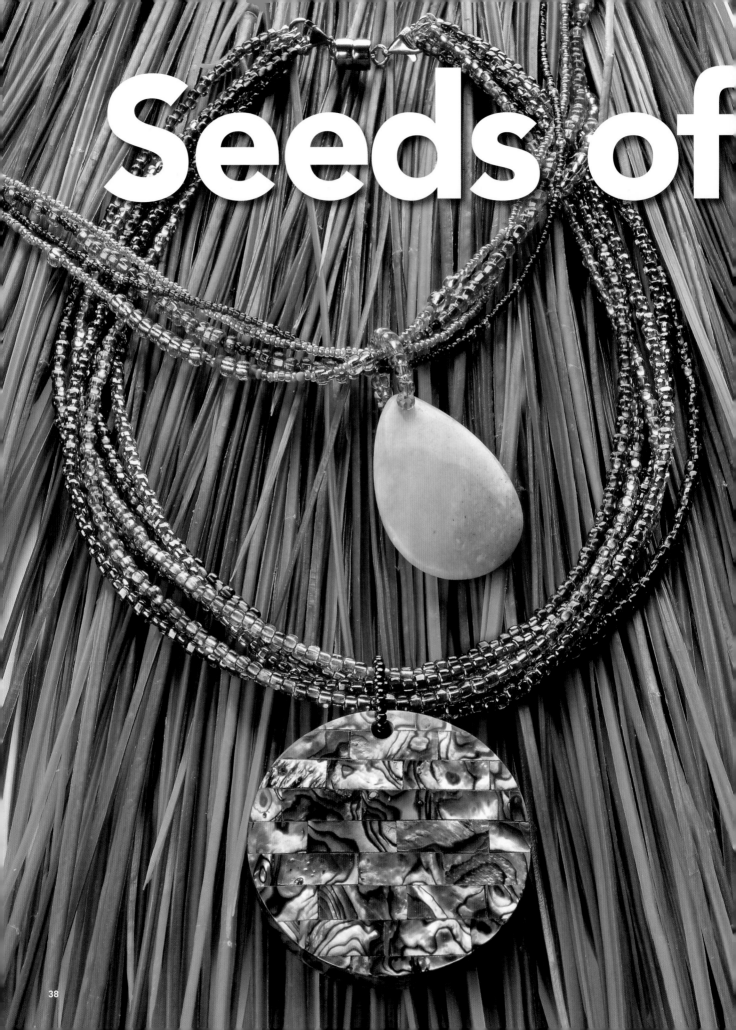

Seeds of

change

by Karli Sullivan

A combination of magnetic and lobster claw clasps and a collection of seed bead strands let you quickly change your color scheme to suit any outfit or pendant. The number of strands you string is up to you, but once you see this project's potential, you'll want one in every color.

Supply List

- pendant with large hole or bail to accommodate seed bead strands
- 2g 11º or 4g 8º seed beads per strand
- flexible beading wire, .014 or .015
- **2** 5mm inside diameter (ID) soldered jump rings per strand
- **2** 4mm ID jump rings
- **2** crimp beads per strand
- magnetic clasp
- **2** lobster claw clasps
- chainnose or crimping pliers
- diagonal wire cutters

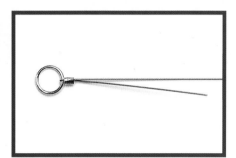

1 Determine the finished length of your necklace. (My necklaces are 19 in./48cm.) Add 6 in. (15cm) and cut a piece of beading wire to that length. String a crimp bead and a soldered jump ring. Go back through the crimp bead and tighten the wire. Crimp the crimp bead (Basics, p. 12).

2 String seed beads, covering the wire tail. Continue to string seed beads until the strand is within 1 in. (2.5cm) of the desired length.

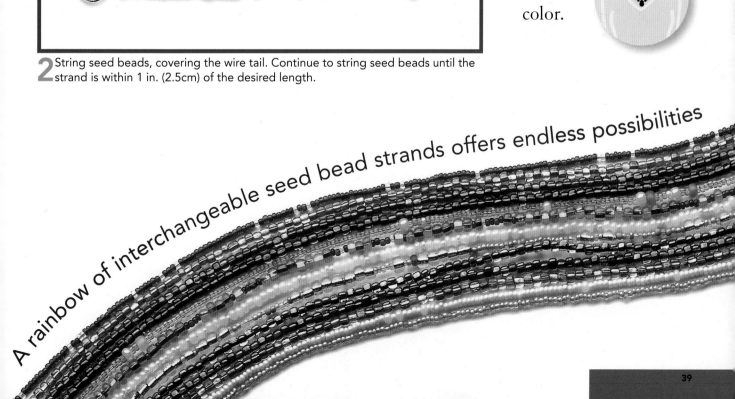

A rainbow of interchangeable seed bead strands offers endless possibilities

3 String a crimp bead and a soldered jump ring. Go back through the last few beads strung and tighten the wire. Check the fit, and add or remove beads if necessary. Crimp the crimp bead and trim the excess wire. Repeat steps 1–3 for each additional strand.

4 Open a jump ring (Basics). Attach a lobster claw clasp and half of a magnetic clasp. Close the jump ring. Repeat with the other half of the magnetic clasp and another lobster claw clasp.

5 Center a pendant over the desired number of strands.
   Attach each end of each strand to one of the lobster claw clasps. ❖

DESIGN GUIDELINES
• To make a seed bead bail, string seed beads, a pendant, and a crimp bead on a 6-in. (15cm) piece of beading wire. Go through the crimp bead and several adjacent beads. Tighten the wire. Crimp the crimp bead (Basics, p. 12) and trim the excess wire.
   • Incorporate small beads or crystals in each strand to add texture and sparkle.

Shortcuts

Readers' tips to make your beading life easier

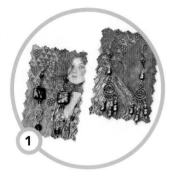

1 postcard display

To display earrings, cut postcards and poke two holes in each piece for the earring wires. If you plan to sell the earrings, write the price on the bottom of the card. The price can be cut off if the earrings are given as a gift.
– Ami Coulliard, Milwaukee, Wis.

2 traveling clipboard

Buy a plastic clipboard that opens to store papers. Inside, place a bead mat to use as a work surface. Then, cover unfinished projects, supplies, and tools with another bead mat. When the clipboard is closed, the contents won't move around.
– Danielle Blumenberg, Orange Park, Fla.

3 conversation piece

I sometimes break beads when I use a bead reamer. Also, when I buy beads in bulk, some strands have broken beads. Instead of wasting these beautiful pieces, I display them in a crystal goblet. The goblet makes a colorful conversation piece.
– Naomi Kuritzky Regan, Bellevue, Wash.

4 fleece mats

I cut a yard of polar fleece into various sizes and use some pieces as work surfaces, some to line baskets that I put beads in, and some to line the drawers of my rolling cart to prevent my tools from sliding when I open the drawer. I also roll my unfinished stringing project in fleece and then tie it with a ribbon to transport it. The lightweight fleece provides a protective surface for the stones.
– Cheryl Finley, via e-mail

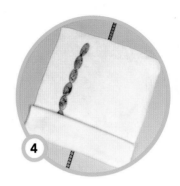

5 earring trees

Small artificial trees are a great way to display earrings. They are usually on sale after the holidays. The ones that have fiber-optic branches are especially beautiful.
– Marcy Whiteside, Delta Junction, Ariz.

Pearls

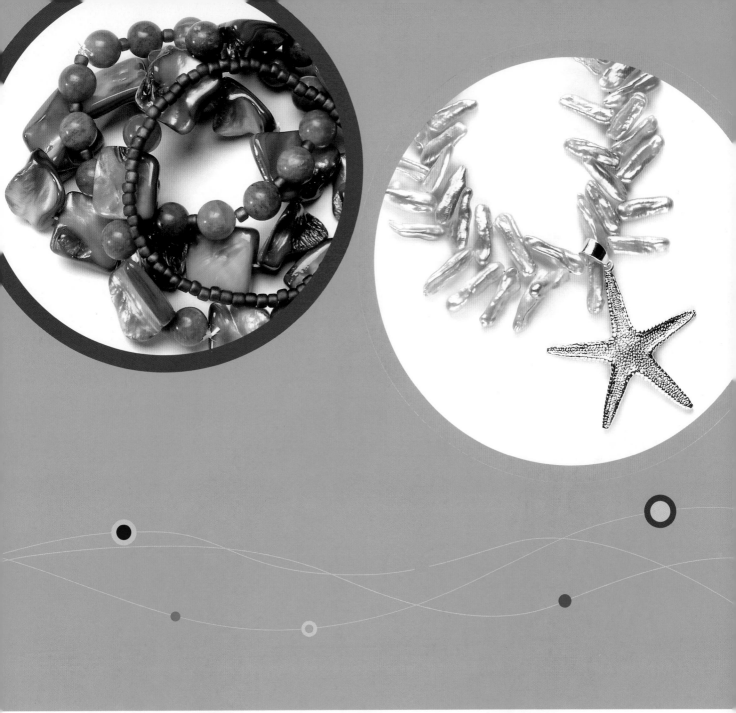

and shells

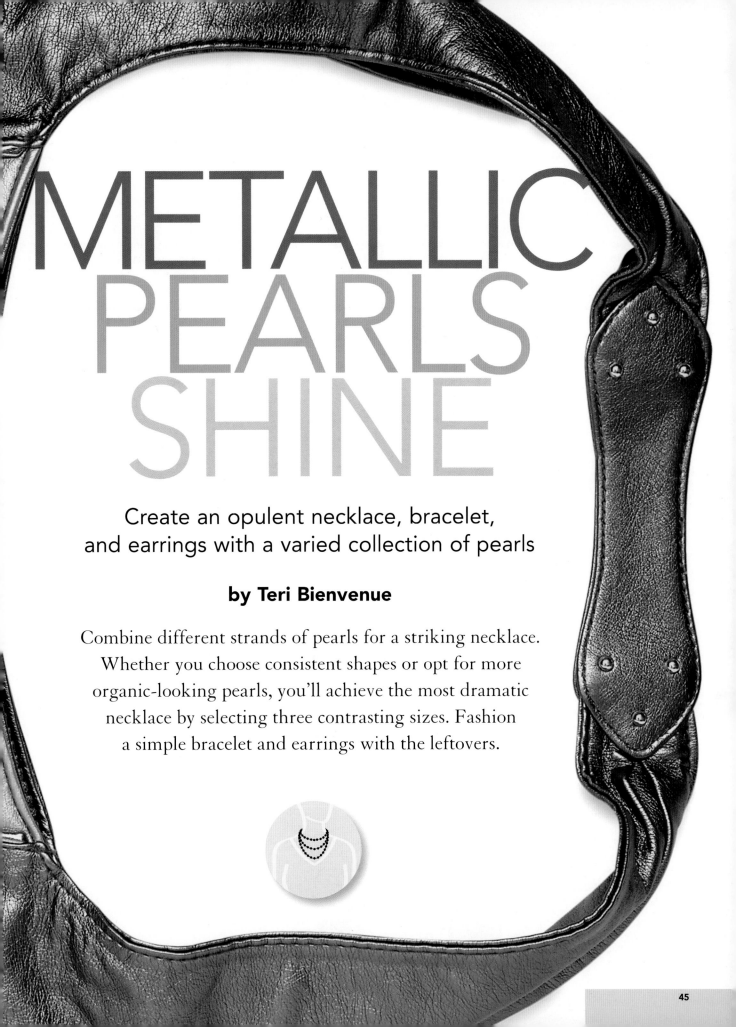

METALLIC
PEARLS
SHINE

Create an opulent necklace, bracelet,
and earrings with a varied collection of pearls

by Teri Bienvenue

Combine different strands of pearls for a striking necklace.
Whether you choose consistent shapes or opt for more
organic-looking pearls, you'll achieve the most dramatic
necklace by selecting three contrasting sizes. Fashion
a simple bracelet and earrings with the leftovers.

1 necklace • For the three large-pearl strands: Cut a piece of beading wire (Basics, p. 12) for the shortest strand of your necklace. (My shortest strands are 15½–20½ in./39.4–52.1cm.) Cut two more pieces, each 4 in. (10cm) longer than the previous piece. On each wire, string large pearls until the strand is within 4 in. (10cm) of the desired length.

2 For the three small-pearl strands: Cut a piece of beading wire 2 in. (5cm) longer than the shortest wire in step 1. Cut two more pieces, each 1 in. (2.5cm) longer than the previous piece. On each wire, string small pearls until the strand is within 4 in. (10cm) of the desired length.

3 For the three medium-pearl strands: Cut a piece of beading wire 4 in. (10cm) longer than the shortest wire in step 1. Cut two more pieces, each 2 in. (5cm) longer than the previous piece. On each wire, string medium pearls until the strand is within 4 in. (10cm) of the desired length.

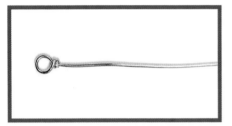

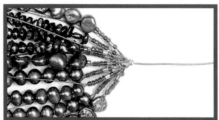

4 Cut a 4-in. (10cm) piece of 20-gauge wire. Make a wrapped loop (Basics) on one end. Repeat.

5 On one end of each strand, string five or six 11º seed beads, a crimp bead, an 11º, and a wrapped loop. Go back through the last few beads strung and tighten the wire. Repeat on the other side. Check the fit, and add or remove beads if necessary, allowing approximately 2 in. (5cm) for finishing. Crimp the crimp beads (Basics) and trim the excess wire.

6 On each end, string a cone, a bead cap, an accent bead, and a bead cap. Make the first half of a wrapped loop. Attach half of a clasp and complete the wraps.

1 bracelet • Cut a piece of beading wire (Basics, p. 12). Center three pearls on the wire.

2 On each end, string: 11º seed bead, bead cap, accent bead, bead cap, 11º, three pearls. Repeat until the strand is within 1 in. (2.5cm) of the desired length.

3 On each end, string a spacer, a crimp bead, a spacer, and half of a clasp. Check the fit, and add or remove beads if necessary. Go back through the beads just strung and tighten the wire. Crimp the crimp bead (Basics) and trim the excess wire.

SUPPLY NOTE
Find the brown clasp at Ancient Moon Beads, 617-926-1887, and the blue clasp at Jess Imports, 415-626-1433. The cones are from Eclectica, 262-641-0910.

Supply List

necklace
- **4** 16-in. (41cm) strands 8–10mm pearls
- **4** 16-in. (41cm) strands 5–6mm pearls
- **4** 16-in. (41cm) strands 2–4mm pearls
- **2** 6–10mm accent beads
- **1g** 11º seed beads
- **4** bead caps
- flexible beading wire, .012 or .013
- **8** in. (20cm) 20-gauge half-hard wire
- **18** crimp beads
- **2** 25–35mm cones
- box clasp
- chainnose and roundnose pliers
- diagonal wire cutters
- crimping pliers (optional)

bracelet
- **13–17** 8–10mm pearls
- **4–6** 6–10mm accent beads
- **8–12** 11º seed beads
- **4** 3–4mm spacers
- **8–12** bead caps
- flexible beading wire, .012 or .013
- **2** crimp beads
- toggle clasp
- chainnose or crimping pliers
- diagonal wire cutters

earrings
- **2** 8–10mm pearls
- **2** 5–6mm pearls
- **2** 6–10mm accent beads
- **1½** in. (3.8cm) chain, 4–5mm links
- **6** 1½-in. (3.8cm) head pins
- pair of decorative earring wires
- chainnose and roundnose pliers
- diagonal wire cutters

1 **earrings •** On a head pin, string a small pearl. Make the first half of a wrapped loop (Basics, p. 12). Repeat with an accent bead and a large pearl.

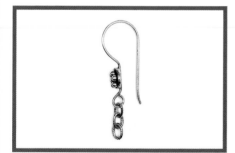

2 Cut a three-link section of chain. Open the loop of an earring wire (Basics). Attach the chain and close the loop.

3 Attach one bead unit to each link and complete the wraps. Make a second earring to match the first. ❖

EDITOR'S TIP
When selecting cones for the necklace, note the size of the bottom opening: it must accommodate nine strands of seed beads.

Beads echo a painter's pal

Choose colors to complement a handpainted shell pendant

by Monica Han

Summer styling is easy with a set that takes under an hour to make. In the necklace, a single strand blooms with beads in colors that match the pendant's details. Pair the necklace with shell dangle earrings, or use any combination of leftover beads to make simple drops. For the best selection, use round gemstone or dyed mother-of-pearl beads.

1 necklace • Open a jump ring (Basics, p. 12). Attach a pendant and the loop of a bail. Close the jump ring. Cut a piece of beading wire (Basics). (My necklaces are 18 in./46cm.) Center the bail on the wire.

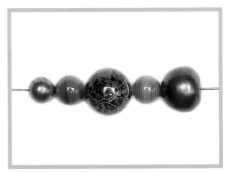

2 On each end, string: 3–4mm pearl, 4mm round bead, 8mm round bead, 4mm round in a second color, 7–8mm pearl. Repeat until the strand is within 1 in. (2.5cm) of the finished length.

EDITOR'S TIP
For a pared-down look, wear the necklace showing the unpainted side of the pendant.

3 On each end, string a round spacer, a crimp bead, a round spacer, and half of a clasp. Check the fit, and add or remove beads from each end if necessary. Go back through the beads just strung and tighten the wire. Crimp the crimp bead (Basics) and trim the excess wire.

ette

1 earrings • On a head pin, string a round bead. Make a plain loop (Basics, p. 12).

2 Cut a 1-in. (2.5cm) piece of chain. Open the loop of the bead unit (Basics) and attach the chain. Close the loop.

3 Open the loop of an earring wire (Basics). Attach the dangle and a shell bead, and close the loop. Make a second earring to match the first. ❖

Supply List

necklace
- 40–50mm shell pendant (Monica Han, mhan@dreambeads.biz)
- **14–16** 8mm round beads
- **28–32** 4mm round beads, in two colors
- **14–16** 7–8mm pearls
- **14–16** 3–4mm pearls
- **4** 3mm round spacers
- flexible beading wire, .014 or .015
- 5–7mm tube bail with loop (Eclectica, 262-641-0910)
- 6–8mm jump ring

- **2** crimp beads
- box clasp
- chainnose and roundnose pliers
- diagonal wire cutters
- crimping pliers (optional)

earrings
- **2** 16–20mm teardrop shell beads
- **2** 5mm round beads
- 2 in. (5cm) chain, 2–3mm links
- **2** 1½-in. (3.8cm) head pins
- pair of earring wires
- chainnose and roundnose pliers
- diagonal wire cutters

Cluster natural & faux finds in organic jewelry

Charms mix swimmingly in a distinctive necklace and earrings

by Brenda Schweder

Display the sea's bounty with a necklace and earrings in blue and green hues. Suspend sunken treasures — like fish charms and weathered coins — from a shell hoop. And try wrapping a floral leaf to make a charm. To play up the natural, no-two-alike look, use different charms in the earrings.

Supply List

necklace

- shell hoop, approximately 50mm
- shell pendant, approximately 60mm
- 50–60mm silk leaf with wire stem
- 20–25mm coin, center drilled
- 2 15–25mm charms
- 2 16-in. (41cm) strands 4mm Czech glass rondelles
- **13–20** 3mm round Czech fire-polished crystals
- flexible beading wire, .014 or .015
- 12 in. (30cm) waxed linen cord, 1mm diameter
- 2 1½-in. (3.8cm) decorative head pins
- **3** 8–10mm jump rings
- 2 crimp beads
- 2 crimp covers
- lobster claw clasp and soldered jump ring
- chainnose and roundnose pliers
- diagonal wire cutters
- crimping pliers (optional)

earrings

- **2** shell pendants, approximately 60mm
- **2** 15–25mm charms
- **6** 3mm round Czech fire-polished crystals
- 12 in. (30cm) waxed linen cord, 1mm diameter
- pair of earring wires
- chainnose pliers

EDITOR'S TIP
Pick up silk leaves at your local craft or floral-supply store. Look for leaves with a wire stem.

1 necklace • On a decorative head pin, make a wrapped loop (Basics, p. 12). With the stem of a leaf, make a wrapped loop. Do not trim the excess stem.

2 Cut a 6-in. (15cm) piece of waxed linen cord. String a shell pendant and tie a surgeon's knot (Basics). Leave a small loop, and tie a second surgeon's knot. Trim the ends as desired, leaving some excess cord.

3 Cut a 6-in. (15cm) piece of waxed linen cord. Fold it in half. String a coin over both ends. Bring the ends through the loop and tighten. Leave a small loop, and tie a surgeon's knot. Trim the ends as desired, leaving some excess cord.

4 Open a jump ring (Basics). Attach the leaf, the loop of the shell pendant, a charm, and a shell hoop. Close the jump ring.

Use a jump ring to attach a fish charm, the decorative head pin, the loop of the coin, and the shell hoop.

5 Cut a piece of beading wire (Basics). (My necklace is 23 in./58cm.) Attach a jump ring to the shell hoop and center it on the wire.

6 On each end, string rondelles, interspersing them with round crystals, until the strand is within 1 in. (2.5cm) of the finished length.

7 On one end, string a crimp bead, a rondelle, and a lobster claw clasp. Repeat on the other end, substituting a soldered jump ring for the clasp. Check the fit, and add or remove beads from each end if necessary. Go back through the last few beads strung and tighten the wire. Crimp the crimp beads (Basics) and trim the excess wire.

8 Use chainnose pliers to close a crimp cover over each crimp. On a decorative head pin, make the first half of a wrapped loop. Attach it to the soldered jump ring and complete the wraps.

1 **earrings •** Cut a 6-in. (15cm) piece of waxed linen cord. String a shell pendant and tie a surgeon's knot (Basics, p. 12).

2 On one end, string a charm. Leave a small loop, and tie a surgeon's knot with both ends. Do not trim the excess cord.

3 On one end, string a crystal and tie an overhand knot (Basics). On the other end, string two crystals and tie an overhand knot. Trim the ends as desired.

4 Open the loop of an earring wire (Basics). Attach the loop of the dangle and close the earring wire's loop. Make a second earring. ❧

53

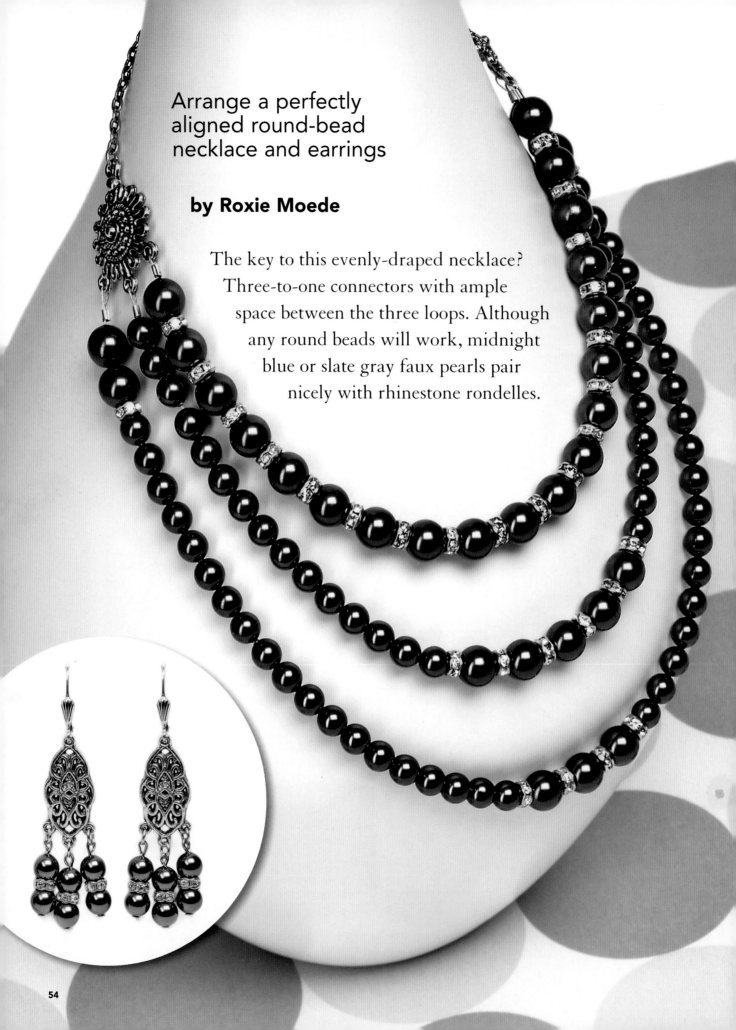

Arrange a perfectly aligned round-bead necklace and earrings

by Roxie Moede

The key to this evenly-draped necklace? Three-to-one connectors with ample space between the three loops. Although any round beads will work, midnight blue or slate gray faux pearls pair nicely with rhinestone rondelles.

3 strands simplified

1 **necklace •** For the beaded section: Cut a piece of beading wire (Basics, p. 12) for the shortest strand. (My shortest strands are 7½ in./19.1cm.) Cut two more pieces, each 2 in. (5cm) longer than the previous piece. Center an 8mm bead on the shortest wire.

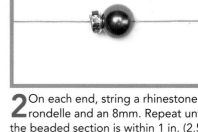

2 On each end, string a rhinestone rondelle and an 8mm. Repeat until the beaded section is within 1 in. (2.5cm) of the desired length.

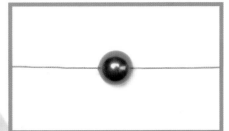

3 On the middle wire, center an alternating pattern of six rondelles and five 8mms.

On each end, string 6mm beads until the beaded section is within 1 in. (2.5cm) of the desired length.

4 On the longest wire, center an alternating pattern of four rondelles and three 8mms.

On each end, string 6mms until the beaded section is within 1 in. (2.5cm) of the desired length. String a rondelle and two 8mms.

SUPPLY NOTE

For three-to-one connectors, check Fire Mountain Gems, 800-355-2137, firemountaingems.com, or Rio Grande, 800-545-6566.

5 On each end, string a spacer, a crimp bead, a spacer, and the corresponding loop of a three-to-one connector. Go back through the last few beads strung, tighten the wire, and crimp the crimp bead (Basics). Trim the excess wire.

6 Decide how long you want the chain section of your necklace to be. (The chain sections of mine are 5½ in./14cm.) Cut a piece of chain to that length, then cut the chain in half. On each end, open a 4mm jump ring (Basics) and attach a chain and the remaining loop of a connector. Close the jump ring.

7 Check the fit, allowing 1 in. (2.5cm) for finishing. Trim chain from each end, if necessary. On one end, use a 4mm jump ring to attach a chain and a lobster claw clasp. Repeat on the other end, substituting a soldered jump ring for the clasp.

1 **earrings •** On a head pin, string a 6mm bead, a rhinestone rondelle, and a 6mm bead. Make a plain loop (Basics, p. 12). Make three bead units.

2 Open a 4mm jump ring (Basics) and attach a bead unit and a loop of a three-to-one connector. Close the jump ring. Use jump rings to attach the remaining bead units.

3 Open the loop of an earring wire (Basics). Attach the dangle and close the loop. Make a second earring to match the first. ❖

Cluster pearls
&crystals

Attach jewel-toned
pearls and crystals to
chain for a Y-necklace
and earrings

by Lanie Ketcherside

Create a flourish of
pearls and crystals
on a shapely chain
necklace. Add
earrings, and you'll have
the trimmings to highlight
a holiday outfit.

1 necklace • String a pearl or crystal on a head pin. Make the first half of a wrapped loop (Basics, p. 12). Make a total of 30 to 35 bead units. Set one unit aside for step 9.

Complete the wraps on two 8mm-pearl units, two 6mm-pearl units, four 4mm-pearl units, and eight crystal units. Set these units aside for steps 5 and 6.

2 Cut a 1-in. (2.5cm) piece of chain. Attach an 8mm unit to a link and complete the wraps. Repeat, attaching two or three bead units to each link.

SupplyList

necklace
- **16–20** 8mm pearls
- **16–20** 6mm pearls
- **16–20** 4mm pearls
- **18–24** 4mm round crystals
- 4 in. (10cm) 26-gauge half-hard wire
- 10–14 in. (25–36cm) chain, 3–4mm links
- **30–35** 1½-in. (3.8cm) 26-gauge head pins
- flexible beading wire, .014 or .015
- **2** crimp beads
- **2** crimp covers (optional)
- lobster claw clasp
- chainnose and roundnose pliers
- diagonal wire cutters
- crimping pliers (optional)

earrings
- **6** 4–8mm pearls
- **4** 4mm round crystals
- **2** in. (5cm) chain, 3–4mm links
- **10** 1½-in. (3.8cm) 26-gauge head pins
- **2** 3–4mm jump rings
- pair of earring wires
- chainnose and roundnose pliers
- diagonal wire cutters

EDITOR'S TIP

Consider closing a crimp cover over each crimp bead. Crimp covers give a polished appearance to a finished necklace, particularly when the crimp beads are located at the front of the necklace.

3 Cut a 2-in. (5cm) piece of 26-gauge wire. Make the first half of a wrapped loop on one end. Attach the chain and complete the wraps. String an 8mm pearl and make a wrapped loop.

4 Determine the finished length of the beaded section of your necklace. (My necklaces are 18 in./46cm; each has a 7-in./18cm beaded section.) Add 6 in. (15cm) and cut a piece of beading wire to that length. Center the chain dangle on the wire. Cut two 4–6-in. (10–15cm) pieces of chain.

5 On each end of the wire, string: crystal, two crystal units, crystal, 8mm unit, crystal, crystal unit.

6 On each end, string: 6mm unit, crystal unit, 8mm pearl, 6mm pearl, 4mm unit, 4mm pearl, 8mm pearl, 4mm pearl, 4mm unit.

7 On each end, string: 6mm pearl, 8mm pearl, 6mm pearl, 4mm pearl, 8mm pearl, 4mm pearl. Repeat until the beaded section is within 1 in. (2.5cm) of the desired length.

8 On each end, string a crystal, a crimp bead, and a chain. Check the fit, allowing 1½ in. (3.8cm) for finishing. Trim chain if necessary. Go back through the beads just strung and tighten the wire. Crimp the crimp bead (Basics) and trim the excess wire. Close a crimp cover over the crimp bead, if desired.

9 Cut a 2-in. (5cm) piece of 26-gauge wire. Make the first half of a wrapped loop, and attach a chain. Complete the wraps. String a crystal and make the first half of a wrapped loop. Attach a lobster claw clasp and complete the wraps.

On the remaining end, attach a bead unit and complete the wraps.

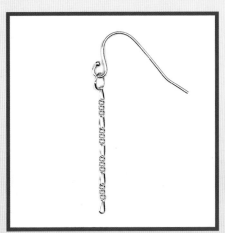

1 **earrings** • Cut a 1-in. (2.5cm) piece of chain. Open a jump ring (Basics, p. 12) and attach an earring wire and the chain. Close the jump ring.

2 Make three pearl units and two crystal units as in step 1 of the necklace. Attach each unit to a link of chain and complete the wraps. Make a second earring to match the first. ❖

Wire wrap
a toggle clasp

Shape your
own clasp and
earrings with this
versatile technique

by Monica Han

For a custom touch, add a handmade toggle clasp to a Swarovski pearl bracelet. You can make a clasp with other 4mm round beads; just make sure the holes are large enough to accommodate 22-gauge wire. Make two more loops to wear as earrings.

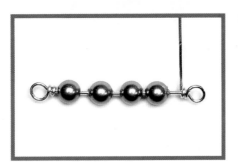

1 bracelet • To make the bar half of a pearl toggle clasp: Cut a 10-in. (25cm) piece of 22-gauge wire. Make a wrapped loop (Basics, p. 12) on one end. String four 4mm round pearls and make a wrapped loop approximately 1 in. (2.5cm) from the first loop. Do not trim the excess wire. (There should be gaps between the pearls.)

2 Wrap the wire around each of the next two pearls. Make a wrapped loop perpendicular to the row of pearls. Do not trim the excess wire.

3 Wrap the wire around the remaining two pearls as in step 2. Wrap the wire around the wraps of the end loop. Trim the excess wire.

4 To make the loop half of the clasp: Cut a 12-in. (30cm) piece of 22-gauge wire. Make a right-angle bend 1½ in. (3.8cm) from one end. On the working end, string eight 4mm pearls. Wrap the wire end around the stem once or twice, making a circle approximately ⅝ in. (1.6cm) in diameter. (There should be gaps between the pearls.)

5 Wrap the wire around the top of the wire circle once or twice. Wrap the wire around each pearl. Make one or two wraps at the top of the circle.

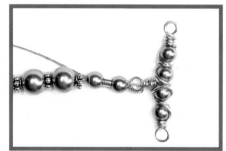

6 Wrap the wire around the stem three or four times. With the stem, make the first half of a wrapped loop.

7 Wrap both wires around the stem (over the wraps made in step 6). Trim the excess wire.

8 Cut a piece of beading wire (Basics). Center a bead cap, a 10mm pearl, and a bead cap on the wire.

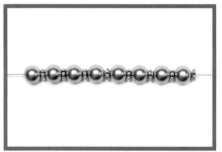

9 On each end, string a 6mm pearl and a flat spacer. Repeat until the bracelet is within 2 in. (5cm) of the finished length.

10 On each end, string a 4mm pearl, a crimp bead, a 4mm pearl, and half of the clasp. Check the fit, and add or remove beads from each end if necessary. Go back through the beads just strung and tighten the wire. Crimp the crimp bead (Basics) and trim the excess wire.

SUPPLY NOTE
All supplies for these projects are available from Artbeads.com, 866-715-2323.

Supply List

bracelet
- 10mm round pearl
- **16–20** 6mm round pearls
- **16** 4mm round pearls
- **16–20** 4–5mm flat spacers
- **2** 7–9mm bead caps
- flexible beading wire, .014 or .015
- 22 in. (56cm) 22-gauge half-hard wire
- **2** crimp beads
- chainnose and roundnose pliers
- diagonal wire cutters
- crimping pliers (optional)

earrings
- **16** 4mm round pearls
- 24 in. (61cm) 22-gauge half-hard wire
- pair of earring wires
- chainnose and roundnose pliers
- diagonal wire cutters

earrings • Follow steps 4–7 of the bracelet. Open the loop of an earring wire (Basics, p. 12) and attach the wrapped loop. Close the earring wire's loop. Make a second earring to match the first. ❖

EDITOR'S TIP
If you prefer more uniform wraps, trim the excess wire after you finish step 5. Then, make a wrapped loop with the remaining wire stem.

STICK PEARLS
point the way to
SUMMER STYLE

Make a shimmering necklace and earrings

by Irina Miech

For quick jewels, try a necklace strung with herringbone-style stick pearls. This new shape is top drilled on a diagonal, so a herringbone pattern will form when you string multiples. To avoid an overly matched look, make faceted pearl earrings.

1 necklace • Cut a piece of beading wire (Basics, p. 12). (The white necklace is 15½ in./39.4cm; the peach necklace, 16 in./41cm.) Center a pendant on the wire.

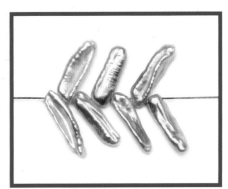

2 On each end, string stick pearls until the necklace is within 1 in. (2.5cm) of the finished length.

3 On one end, string a spacer, a crimp bead, a spacer, and a lobster claw clasp. Repeat on the other end, substituting a 2-in. (5cm) chain for the clasp. Check the fit, and add or remove beads from each end if necessary. Go back through the beads just strung and tighten the wire. Crimp the crimp beads (Basics) and trim the excess wire.

4 On a head pin, string a round pearl. Make the first half of a wrapped loop (Basics). Attach the loop to the chain and complete the wraps.

Supply List

necklace
- 35–45mm pendant (Eclectica, 262-641-0910)
- 16-in. (41cm) strand 14–20mm herringbone-style stick pearls (Eclectica)
- 8–12mm faceted round pearl
- **4** 3mm round spacers
- flexible beading wire, .014 or .015
- 1½-in. (3.8cm) head pin
- **2** crimp beads
- lobster claw clasp
- 2 in. (5cm) chain for extender, 4–5mm links
- chainnose and roundnose pliers
- diagonal wire cutters
- crimping pliers (optional)

earrings
- 2 8–12mm faceted round pearls
- 1¼ in. (3.2cm) chain, 4–5mm links
- 2 1½-in. (3.8cm) head pins
- pair of earring wires
- chainnose and roundnose pliers
- diagonal wire cutters

EDITOR'S TIP
When you buy diagonally drilled stick pearls, they're usually strung in a herringbone pattern. To keep the pattern intact for easy stringing, cut the strand in the center and string the pearls onto each end of your beading wire.

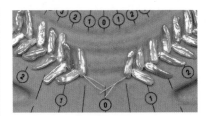

1 earrings • On a head pin, string a pearl. Make the first half of a wrapped loop (Basics, p. 12).

2 Cut a ½-in. (1.3cm) piece of chain. Attach the pearl unit and complete the wraps.

3 Open the loop of an earring wire (Basics) and attach the dangle. Close the loop. Make a second earring to match the first. ❖

Cash in on coin pearls

Lustrous coin-pearl earrings are this season's fashion currency

by Devona J. Jefferson

When you take stock of your earring collection, make sure you have some dressy earrings for the holiday season. These two designs fit the bill nicely, highlighting coin pearls with a cluster of metallic beads or a sweep of chain.

1 **double-pearl earrings** • Using chainnose pliers, bend the tip of a piece of 24-gauge wire back against itself. Trim the wire ¾ in. (1.9cm) from the end. Make 16 decorative wires.

2 String a spacer on a decorative wire. Make a plain loop (Basics, p. 12). Repeat with the remaining wires.

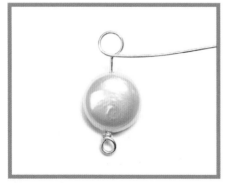

3 On a head pin, string a coin pearl. Make the first half of a wrapped loop (Basics).

4 Attach eight spacer units to the loop. Complete the wraps.

EDITOR'S TIP
Try substituting 32 decorative head pins for 32 in. (81cm) of 24-gauge wire in the double-pearl earrings.

5 Cut a 3-in. (7.6cm) piece of wire. Make a 2mm wrapped loop on one end. String a coin pearl and make the first half of a 3–4mm wrapped loop.

6 Attach eight spacer units to the 3–4mm loop. Complete the wraps.

7 Open a jump ring (Basics). Attach the first bead unit's wrapped loop and the second bead unit's 2mm loop. Close the jump ring. Use a jump ring to attach the dangle and the loop of an earring post. Make a second earring to match the first.

1 **pearl-and-chain earrings •** Cut a 1½-in. (3.8cm) piece of 24-gauge wire. Make a plain loop (Basics, p. 12). String a spacer, a coin pearl, and a spacer. Make a plain loop.

2 Cut a 3-in. (7.6cm) piece of wire. String a large briolette and make a set of wraps (Basics). Make a wrapped loop (Basics) above the wraps. Repeat with two small briolettes.

3 Cut two ⅜-in. (1cm) and one ½-in. (1.3cm) pieces of chain. Open a jump ring (Basics) and attach the longer chain and the loop of the large briolette. Close the jump ring. Use jump rings to attach the remaining chains to the loops of the small briolettes.

4 Use a jump ring to attach the chain dangles to a loop of the coin-pearl unit, stringing the large-briolette dangle in the middle. Close the jump ring.

5 Open the loop of the dangle (Basics). Attach the loop of an earring post. Close the dangle's loop. (If the earring post has a perpendicular loop, attach a jump ring between the dangle and the loop.) Make a second earring to match the first. ❖

The right color and
bead choices
create visual impact

by Teri Bienvenue

A trio of trendy stretch bracelets

Start practicing your multiplication tables, because once you whip through a set of these quick elastic bracelets, you'll want a jewelry box full. When you choose beads in contrasting colors and shapes, simple jewelry will really pop.

1 bracelet • Decide how long you want your bracelet to be, add 3 in. (7.6cm), and cut a piece of ribbon elastic to that length. String 8mm round beads until the bracelet is the finished length.

2 Tie a square knot (Basics, p. 12). Glue the knot and trim the ends. Make two more bracelets using mother-of-pearl nuggets.

EARRING OPTIONS
For a change of pace, string a different-colored nugget at the front of each earring. Or wear just one nugget on each hoop, either in the same or different colors.

1 earrings • On a head pin, string a nugget. Make a wrapped loop (Basics, p. 12). Repeat with a second nugget in a different color.

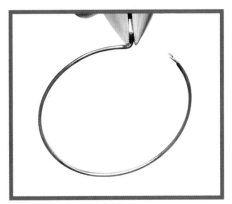

2 On one end of a hoop earring, use chainnose pliers to bend ¼ in. (6mm) of wire up at a right angle.

3 String the nugget units on the hoop. Make a second earring to match the first. ❧

Supply List

All supplies from Fire Mountain Gems, 800-355-2137, firemountaingems.com.

bracelet
• 20–28 10–15mm mother-of-pearl nuggets, in two colors
• 19–25 8mm round beads
• ribbon elastic
• G-S Hypo Cement

earrings
• 4 10–15mm mother-of-pearl nuggets, in two colors
• 4 1½-in. (3.8cm) head pins
• pair of 1-in. (2.5cm) hoop earrings
• chainnose and roundnose pliers
• diagonal wire cutters

EDITOR'S TIPS
• For variety, try different complementary bead mixes or add a seed bead accent bracelet to the trio.
• If you have trouble stringing the ribbon elastic through the mother-of-pearl nuggets, fold a short piece of very fine beading wire in half to make a needle. String the elastic through the wire and pull the wire ends through the nugget.
• You can make two or three bracelets with one 16-in. (41cm) strand of beads.

EDITOR'S TIP

Look to the past for inspiration. Vintage or resale shops and estate or rummage sales are great places to find treasures. Broken jewelry can easily be reconstructed into unique accessories.

1 **necklace** • Cut three pieces of beading wire (Basics, p. 12). (The shell-pendant necklace is 20 in./51cm; the blacklip-pendant necklace, 16 in./ 41cm.) Over all three wires, center a pendant. On each end of each wire, string two spacers.

2 On each end of each wire, string pearls as desired until the strand is within 1 in. (2.5cm) of the finished length.

BIG PENDANTS
pull pearls to the
FASHION FOREFRONT

A bold necklace and earrings make a big impact

by Deborah Tuttle

For up-front fashion, a big pendant says it all. Whether you restring a vintage pendant or incorporate a new one, displaying it with multiple pearl strands amplifies its impact. The subtle color differences between the pearls underscore the pendant's iridescence.

necklace

- 50–80mm pendant (blacklip American Indian headdress from Beads and Pieces, 800-652-3237, beadsandpieces.com)
- **3** 16-in. (41cm) strands 6–10mm pearls, in three colors (Pearlwear, 760-943-7436, pearlwear.com)
- **30** 3mm spacers
- flexible beading wire, .014 or .015
- **6** crimp beads
- toggle clasp
- chainnose or crimping pliers
- diagonal wire cutters

earrings

- **2** charms, approximately 16mm
- **2** 6–10mm pearls
- **8** 3mm spacers
- 5 in. (13cm) 24-gauge wire
- **8** 1½-in. (3.8cm) head pins
- pair of lever-back earring wires
- chainnose and roundnose pliers
- diagonal wire cutters

3 On each end of each strand, string two spacers, a crimp bead, and a spacer. Over all three strands, string half of a clasp. Check the fit, and add or remove beads from each end if necessary. Go back through the beads just strung and tighten the wire. Crimp the crimp bead (Basics) and trim the excess wire.

1 earrings • Cut a 2½-in. (6.4cm) piece of 24-gauge wire. Make the first half of a wrapped loop on one end (Basics, p. 12). Attach a charm and complete the wraps.

2 On a head pin, string a spacer. Make a plain loop (Basics). Make four spacer units.

3 Open the loop of a spacer unit (Basics) and attach the wrapped loop. Close the loop. Repeat to attach the remaining spacer units.

4 String a pearl above the wraps and make a wrapped loop.

5 Open the loop of an earring wire (Basics). Attach the dangle and close the loop. Make a second earring to match the first. ✤

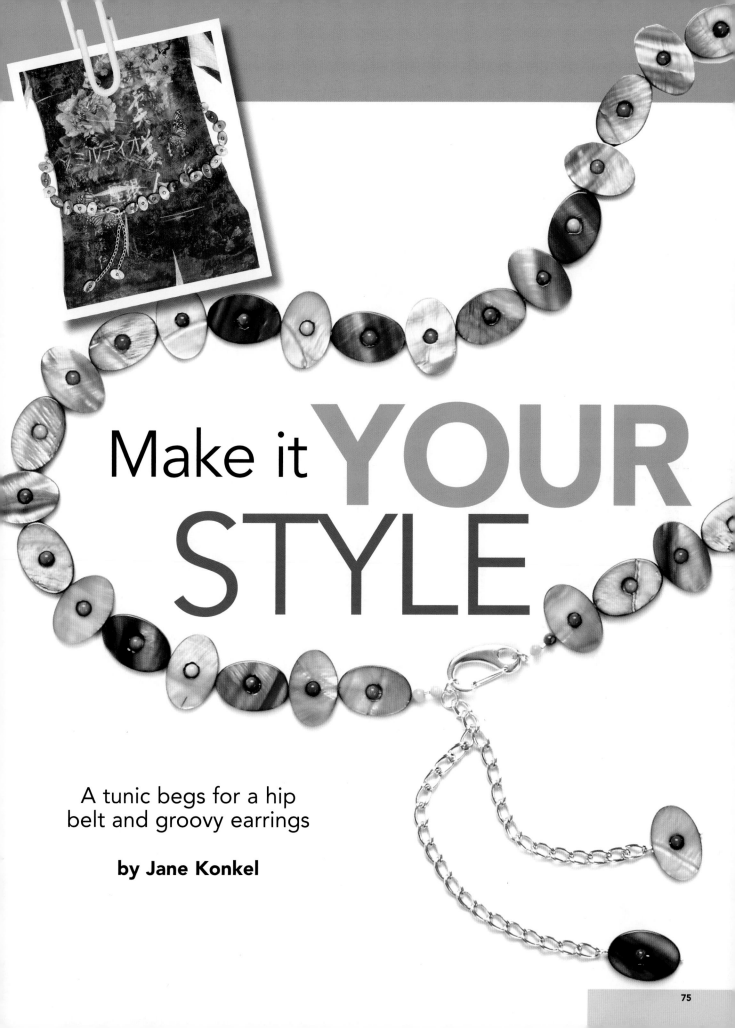

Make it **YOUR** STYLE

A tunic begs for a hip belt and groovy earrings

by Jane Konkel

This tunic's jewel tones match with the organic, pearly sheen of these shells, while the vivid colors in the accent beads provide just the right pop. Find your inspiration piece, and then use your accessories — this great belt and earrings — to make the look your own.

1 **belt** • Measure your hips, add 6 in. (15cm), and cut a piece of beading wire to that length. (My belt is 40 in./1m.) String: one hole of a horizontally drilled donut bead, round bead, remaining hole of the donut, one hole of a vertically drilled donut, round, remaining hole of the donut. Repeat until the strand is within 2 in. (5cm) of the finished length.

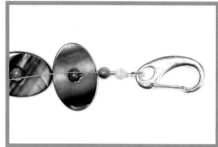

2 Open a jump ring (Basics, p. 12) and attach a lobster-style clasp. Close the jump ring.

On one end, string a round, a crimp bead, a round, and the clasp's jump ring. Go back through the beads just strung and crimp the crimp bead (Basics). Trim the excess wire.

3 On the other end, string a round, a crimp bead, a round, and a jump ring. Check the fit, and add or remove beads if necessary. Go back through the beads just strung and crimp the crimp bead. Trim the excess wire.

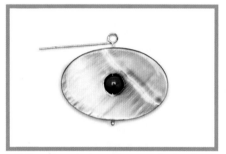

4 On a head pin, string one hole of a horizontal donut, a round, and the remaining hole of the donut. Make the first half of a wrapped loop (Basics). Repeat with a vertical donut.

5 Cut an 8–12-in. (20–30cm) piece of chain. Attach a donut unit to each end of the chain. Complete the wraps.

6 Use a jump ring to attach a link of the chain to the jump ring from step 3, attaching the chain so the donuts hang asymmetrically.

EDITOR'S TIP
If the holes in the beads are large enough, use .018 or .019 beading wire.

1 **earrings** • On a head pin, string one hole of a donut bead, a round bead, and the remaining hole of the donut. Make a wrapped loop (Basics, p. 12).

2 Open an earring wire (Basics) and attach the dangle. Close the wire. Make a second earring to match the first.

Supply List

Shell donuts are available from Eclectica, 262-641-0910.

belt
- **2** 16-in. (41cm) strands 20 x 30mm shell donuts, vertically drilled
- **2** 16-in. (41cm) strands 20 x 30mm shell donuts, horizontally drilled
- **40–50** 5mm round beads, in five colors
- flexible beading wire, .014 or .015
- 8–12 in. (20–30cm) chain, 8–12mm links
- **2** 2½-in. (6.4cm) decorative head pins
- **3** 8mm jump rings

- **2** crimp beads
- key-ring lobster-style clasp, approximately 32mm (JoAnn Stores, joann.com)
- chainnose and roundnose pliers
- diagonal wire cutters
- crimping pliers (optional)

earrings
- **2** 20 x 30mm shell donuts, vertically drilled
- **2** 5mm round beads
- **2** 2½-in. (6.4cm) decorative head pins
- pair of earring wires
- chainnose and roundnose pliers
- diagonal wire cutters

by Sara Strauss

Quick
knots yield a
delicate necklace

1 **necklace** • On one end of a piece of beading cord, tie an overhand knot (Basics, p. 12). String a bead tip. Trim the excess cord and apply glue to the knot. Using chainnose pliers, close the bead tip over the knot.

2 a Tie an overhand knot 1 in. (2.5cm) from the previous knot. String a 5mm pearl, and tie an overhand knot next to the pearl. Repeat with a 3mm pearl.
 b Repeat step 2a until the strand is half of the desired length. (The rectangle-pendant necklace is 18½ in./47cm; the diamond-pendant necklace, 16½ in./41.9cm.)

3 Tie an overhand knot ⅛ in. (3mm) from the previous knot. String a pearl the same size as the previous pearl. Tie an overhand knot next to the pearl.

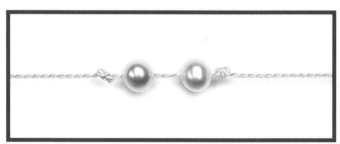

4 Repeat step 2a until the strand is within 1 in. (2.5cm) of the desired length. String a bead tip, and tie an overhand knot 1 in. (2.5cm) from the previous knot. Trim the excess cord and apply glue to the knot. Using chainnose pliers, close the bead tip over the knot.

5 For the second strand, repeat steps 1 and 2a, reversing the pattern of 5mm and 3mm pearls, until the strand is within 1 in. (2.5cm) of half the desired length.
 Tie an overhand knot 1 in. (2.5cm) from the previous knot. String two same-sized pearls, and tie an overhand knot ½ in. (1.3cm) from the previous knot.
 Repeat step 4.

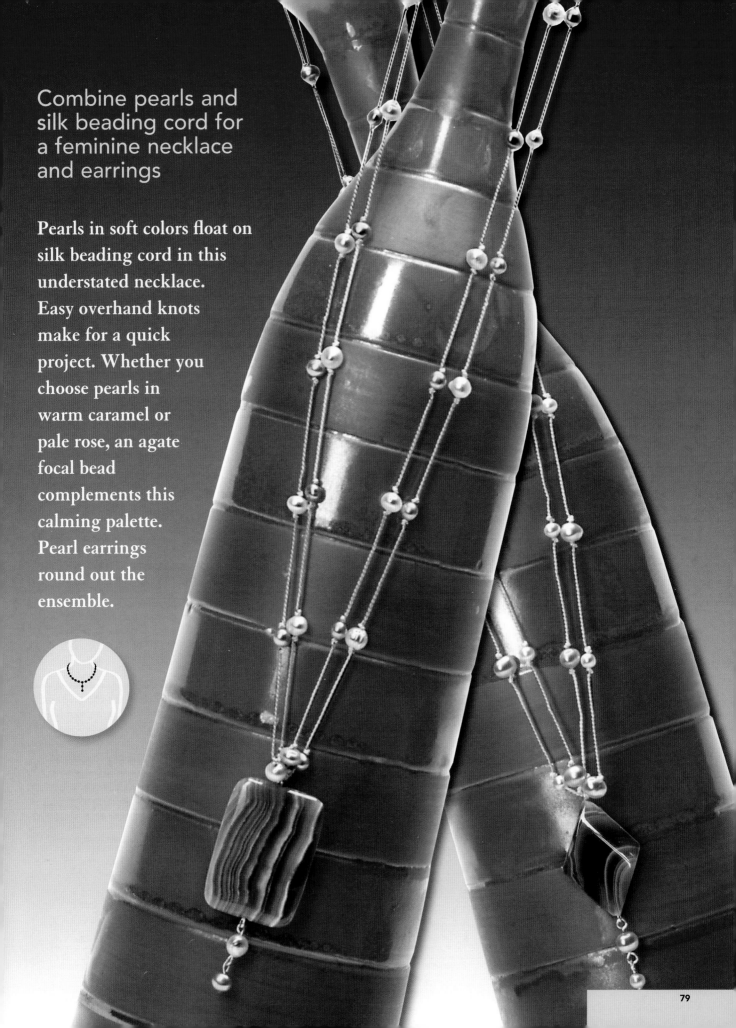

Combine pearls and
silk beading cord for
a feminine necklace
and earrings

Pearls in soft colors float on
silk beading cord in this
understated necklace.
Easy overhand knots
make for a quick
project. Whether you
choose pearls in
warm caramel or
pale rose, an agate
focal bead
complements this
calming palette.
Pearl earrings
round out the
ensemble.

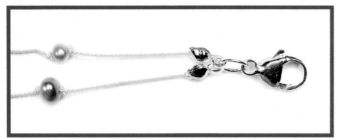

6 On one side, attach the bead tips' loops to a 6mm jump ring. Close the loops. Open the jump ring (Basics) and attach a lobster claw clasp. Close the jump ring.

On the other side, attach the bead tips' loops to a soldered jump ring. Close the loops.

7 On a head pin, string a 3mm pearl. Make a plain loop (Basics).

1 **earrings •** On a head pin, string a 3mm pearl. Make a plain loop (Basics, p. 12).

Supply List

necklace
- gemstone focal bead, approximately 18 x 22mm
- **15–19** 5mm pearls
- **15–19** 3mm pearls
- card of silk beading cord, size 4 or 5
- 3 in. (7.6cm) 24-gauge half-hard wire
- 1-in. (2.5cm) 24-gauge head pin
- 6mm jump ring
- **4** bead tips
- lobster claw clasp and soldered jump ring
- chainnose and roundnose pliers
- diagonal wire cutters
- G-S Hypo Cement

earrings
- **2** 5mm pearls
- **4** 3mm pearls
- 4 in. (10cm) 24-gauge half-hard wire
- **2** 1-in. (2.5cm) 24-gauge head pins
- pair of earring wires
- chainnose and roundnose pliers
- diagonal wire cutters

8 Cut a 1-in. (2.5cm) piece of wire and make a plain loop on one end. String a 5mm pearl and make a plain loop.

Cut a 2-in. (5cm) piece of wire and make a plain loop on one end. String a focal bead and make a plain loop.

9 Open the loops (Basics) of the 5mm-pearl unit. Attach the 3mm-pearl unit to one loop and the focal-bead unit to the other. Close the loops.

Open the dangle's loop and attach it to the center of both necklace strands. Close the loop.

2 Cut a 1-in. (2.5cm) piece of wire. Make a plain loop on one end. String a 3mm pearl, and make a plain loop. Repeat with a 5mm pearl.

3 Open the loops (Basics) of the 5mm-pearl unit and attach a 3mm-pearl unit to each loop. Close the loops.

Open the loop of an earring wire (Basics) and attach the dangle. Close the loop. Make a second earring to match the first. ❖

Shortcuts

Readers' tips to make your beading life easier

1 safety pin security

I often misplace my crimp beads or mistakenly use them instead of small metal beads. To identify them more easily, I thread them onto a safety pin. I can always find the safety pin.
– *Kasey Ford, West Hills, Calif.*

2 tie-rack tip

Do you have an old tie rack lying around that you're not using? Turn it into a space-saving display for your necklaces. The pictured tie rack is available from Linens 'n Things, lnt.com. You can also buy one at a discount store. It rotates, has plenty of hooks, and easily mounts on the wall.
– *Denise Kalanj, via e-mail*

3 tiny storage

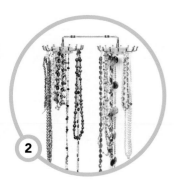

Breath-mint boxes make wonderful storage containers for seed beads, findings, or special small beads. The lid snaps tightly into place, so there's no threat of the beads spilling out. Put a white sticky label on the front to identify its contents.
– *Linda Siegel, Chalfont, Pa.*

4 terra-cotta saucers

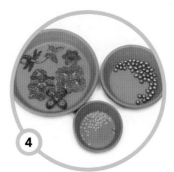

Terra-cotta pottery saucers work great for holding beads. The heavy base makes them less likely to be knocked over, and you can see your beads at a glance.
– *Ryann Anderson, via e-mail*

5 stop beads from slipping

It never fails, just as I'm checking the fit of a necklace, I accidentally let go of one end and the beads spill off. So now I use a metal key ring on each end of the beading wire to prevent beads from coming off. The rings are practical and inexpensive.
– *Mollie Chen, Bloomington, Ind.*

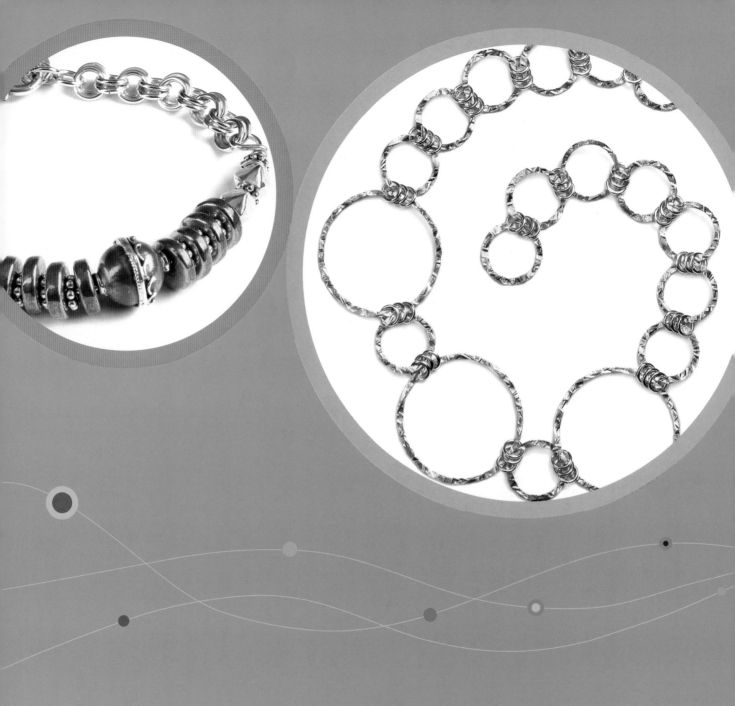

Metal

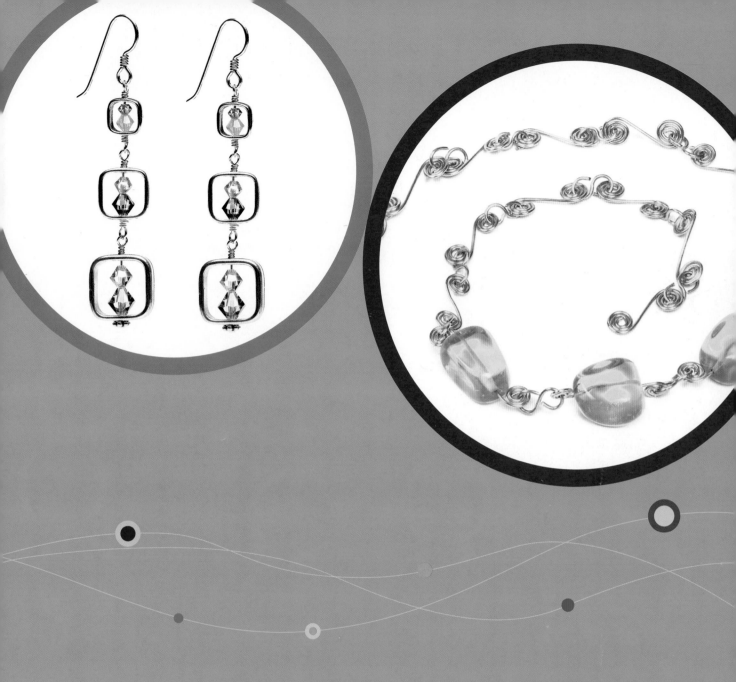

and chain

Moving in fashionable circles

Link hammered hoops into a necklace and earring set

by Heidi Hermreck

Join different-sized silver and gold hoops with jump rings to keep in step with today's mixed-metals trend. The hoops have an eye-catching hammered texture that needs no embellishment. If you want a touch of color, add bead dangles to a pair of earrings to bring this fashion-forward look full circle.

SupplyList

• To make the necklace and earrings on page 84, substitute silver for gold and gold for silver in the supply list and instructions.
• All supplies are available from Via Murano, (877) 842-6872, viamurano.com.

necklace
• 3 44mm silver hoops
• **13–17** 21mm gold hoops
• **33–37** 8mm silver jump rings
• **16–20** 8mm gold jump rings
• 14mm lobster claw clasp
• **2** pairs of chainnose pliers or chainnose and roundnose pliers

bead-and-hoop earrings
• **2** 27mm gold hoops
• **2** 13mm metal beads
• **4** 6mm bicone crystals
• **4** 4mm bicone crystals
• **6** 2-in. (5cm) gold head pins
• **6** 6mm gold jump rings
• pair of gold earring wires
• chainnose and roundnose pliers
• diagonal wire cutters
• additional chainnose pliers (optional)

two-hoop earrings
• **4** 21mm gold hoops
• **6** 8mm silver jump rings
• **4** 8mm gold jump rings
• pair of gold earring wires
• **2** pairs of chainnose pliers or chainnose and roundnose pliers

1 necklace • Open a gold jump ring (Basics, p. 12). Attach a silver hoop and a gold hoop. Close the jump ring. Attach a silver jump ring on each side of the gold jump ring.

2 Repeat step 1 to attach another gold hoop to the silver hoop.

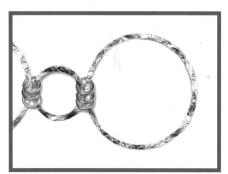

3 On each end, use a gold jump ring and two silver jump rings to attach a silver hoop.

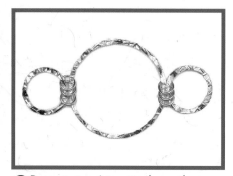

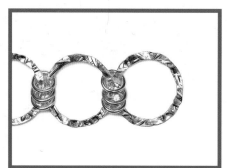

4 On each end, use a gold jump ring and two silver jump rings to attach gold hoops until the necklace is within 2 in. (5cm) of the finished length. (My necklace is 18½ in./47cm.) End with a gold hoop.

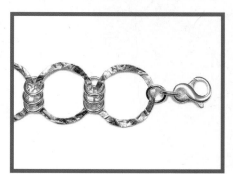

5 On one end, attach a silver jump ring, a gold jump ring, and a lobster claw clasp. On the other end, use a gold jump ring and two silver jump rings to attach a gold hoop as in step 4.

1 **bead-and-hoop earrings •** On a head pin, string a 4mm bicone crystal, a metal bead, and a 4mm bicone. Make a wrapped loop (Basics, p. 12).

2 On a head pin, string a 6mm bicone crystal. Make a wrapped loop. Repeat.

3 Open a jump ring (Basics). Attach the bead units and a hoop. Close the jump ring.

4 Use two jump rings to attach the dangle and the loop of an earring wire. Make a second earring to match the first.

1 **two-hoop earrings •** Open a gold jump ring (Basics, p. 12). Attach two hoops. Close the jump ring.

2 Attach a silver jump ring on each side of the gold jump ring.

3 Attach a silver jump ring to one hoop. Use a gold jump ring to attach the silver jump ring and the loop of an earring wire. Make a second earring to match the first. ❖

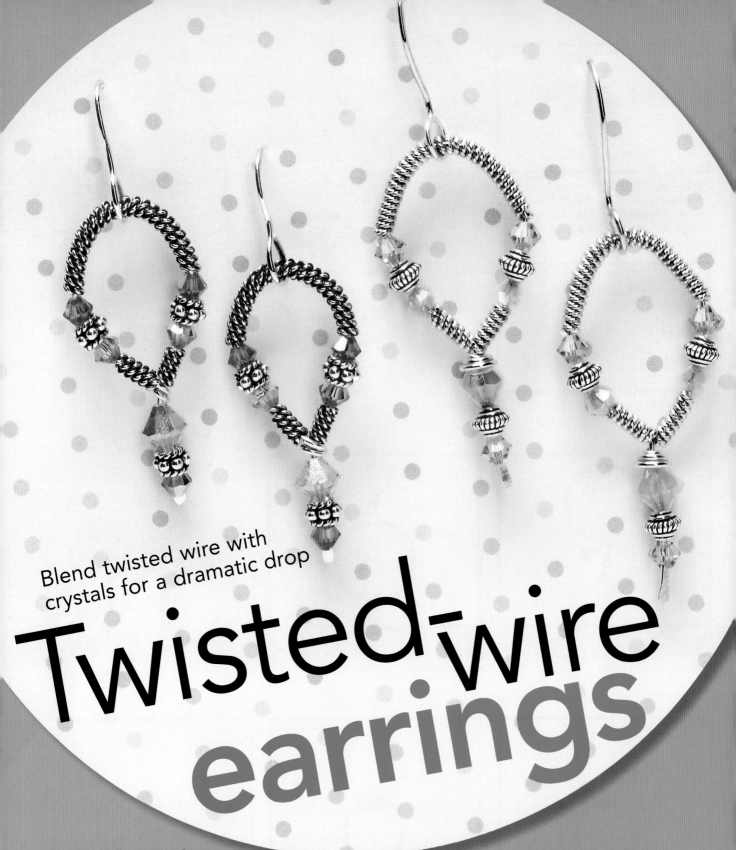

Blend twisted wire with
crystals for a dramatic drop

Twisted-wire
earrings

by Wendy Witchner

With the right tools, these teardrop earrings are a breeze to make. Provide sparkling accents with bicone crystals, or try small gemstones. Just be sure the holes of your beads are large enough to accommodate 20-gauge wire.

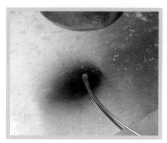

1 Cut a 5-in. (13cm) piece of 20-gauge wire. On a bench block or anvil, hammer approximately ⅛ in. (3mm) of one end. File the end, if necessary.

2 String a 4mm color A bicone crystal, a spacer, and a 6mm bicone crystal. Make a right-angle bend.

3 To make a coil: Cut a 2-in. (5cm) piece of twisted wire. Wrap one end around the tip of your roundnose pliers twice. String the twisted wire on the 20-gauge wire. Gripping the twisted wire with crimping pliers, wrap the wire to make a ¼-in. (6mm) coil. Trim the excess twisted wire.

4 String a 4mm color B bicone crystal, a spacer, and a color A bicone. Cut a 4-in. (10cm) piece of twisted wire. Make a coil approximately 1 in. (2.5cm) long. Trim the excess twisted wire. String a color A bicone, a spacer, and a color B bicone.

5 Cut a 2-in. (5cm) piece of twisted wire. Make a ¼-in. (6mm) coil. Wrap the beaded wire around a cylindrical object, like a pen barrel, forming a teardrop shape. With the remaining 20-gauge wire, make a set of wraps above the 6mm bicone. Trim the excess wire.

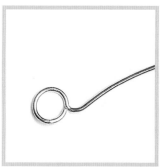

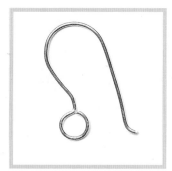

6 To make an earring wire: Cut a 2½-in. (6.4cm) piece of 20-gauge wire. Using the largest part of your round-nose pliers, make a plain loop (Basics, p. 12). Make a slight bend above the loop.

7 Approximately ½ in. (1.3cm) from the bend, form the wire around the cylindrical object. Using chainnose pliers, bend the end of the wire upward. File the end if necessary.

8 Open the loop of the earring wire (Basics) and attach the dangle. Close the loop. Make a second earring to match the first. ✤

Supply List

- **2** 6mm bicone crystals
- **10** 4mm bicone crystals, **6** in color A and **4** in color B
- **6** 5mm spacers
- 15 in. (38cm) 20-gauge half-hard wire
- 16 in. (41cm) 20-gauge twisted wire
- chainnose and round nose pliers
- crimping pliers
- diagonal wire cutters
- bench block or anvil
- hammer
- pen or other cylindrical object
- metal file or emery board (optional)

Chain male bracelet

by Steven James

Link nuggets and jump rings into a heavy bracelet

Combine gemstones with simple Byzantine chain mail for a stylish, masculine bracelet. Tektites (glassy stones formed by a meteorite crash) give a rugged feel to the piece while the smooth turquoise option offers a touch of sophistication.

1 Cut a 3-in. (7.6cm) piece of wire. On one end, make a wrapped loop (Basics, p. 12). String one or two gemstone beads and make the first half of a wrapped loop. Make four bead units.

first pair

second pair

2 To make a short chain-mail unit: Open three jump rings (Basics). Attach each to the wrapped loop of a bead unit. Close the jump rings. Attach two jump rings to the group of three and two jump rings to the group of two.

3 Holding the three-jump-ring group with chainnose pliers, let the two pairs of jump rings fall to the sides.

4 Attach a jump ring to the second pair of jump rings, making sure the new jump ring is positioned between the first pair.

5 Attach two more jump rings as in step 4. The pairs of jump rings will splay out as shown.

6 To make a medium chain-mail unit: Follow steps 2–5. Attach two additional jump rings on the end of the unit.

7 To make a long chain-mail unit: Repeat steps 2–5, then repeat steps 3–5. Make a second long unit.

8 Attach a lobster claw clasp to the open loop of the short chain-mail unit. Complete the wraps.

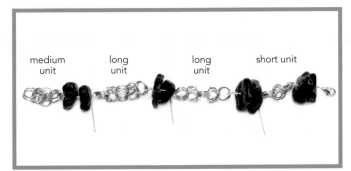

medium unit long unit long unit short unit

9 Attach the loops and the jump rings as shown. Complete the wraps. Check the fit, and add or remove jump rings if necessary. ❖

SupplyList

- **4–10** 14–18mm gemstone beads
- 12–15 in. (30–38cm) 22-gauge half-hard wire
- **57–74** 9mm jump rings
- lobster claw clasp
- **2** pairs of chainnose pliers
- roundnose pliers
- diagonal wire cutters

EDITOR'S TIPS
- Because you'll be opening and closing many jump rings, get a second pair of chainnose pliers to make the job easier.
- If you're making a bracelet more than 10 in. (25cm) long, think about attaching an additional small chain-mail unit.

Frame it FAST

Tiers of framed crystals sparkle in linear earrings

Jenna Colyar-Cooper

Get a jump start on style by bordering sparkling crystals with sterling silver frames. The graduated frame and crystal sizes create a streamlined look that reflects this season's minimalist fashions.

1 On a head pin, string: spacer, one hole of a 14mm frame, 6mm color A crystal, 5mm color B crystal, remaining hole of the frame. Make a wrapped loop (Basics, p. 12).

Supply List

All supplies for this project are available from Fusion Beads, 888-781-3559, fusionbeads.com.

- **2** 6mm bicone crystals, color A
- **4** 5mm bicone crystals, **2** color B, **2** color C
- **4** 4mm bicone crystals, **2** color B, **2** color D
- **2** 3mm bicone crystals, color B
- **2** 14mm bead frames
- **2** 11mm bead frames
- **2** 8mm bead frames
- **2** 3–4mm flat spacers
- 12 in. (30cm) 24-gauge half-hard wire
- **2** 2-in. (5cm) 24-gauge head pins
- pair of earring wires
- chainnose and roundnose pliers
- diagonal wire cutters

2 Cut a 3-in. (7.6cm) piece of wire. On one end, make the first half of a wrapped loop. String one hole of an 11mm frame, a 5mm color C crystal, a 4mm color B crystal, and the remaining hole of the frame. Make the first half of a wrapped loop.

Cut a 3-in. (7.6cm) piece of wire. On one end, make a wrapped loop. String one hole of an 8mm frame, a 4mm color D crystal, a 3mm color B crystal, and the remaining hole of the frame. Make a wrapped loop.

3 Attach the loop of the 14mm-frame unit to the bottom loop of the 11mm-frame unit. Attach the top loop of the 11mm-frame unit to the bottom loop of the 8mm-frame unit. Complete the wraps.

4 Open the loop of an earring wire (Basics). Attach the dangle and close the loop. Make a second earring to match the first. ❖

Link your way to a casual bracelet

Fine chain connects gemstone and metal rings

by Irina Miech

Chain has risen to fashion stardom, but it can still play a supporting role. In this simple bracelet design, delicate chain and wrapped loops link earth-toned gemstones for a great everyday look.

SupplyList

- **5–6** 12mm gemstone rings
- **6–7** 4mm round gemstone beads
- **5–6** 9mm metal rings
- 12–14 in. (30–36cm) 22- or 24-gauge half-hard wire
- 7½–9 in. (19.1–23cm) chain, 2mm links
- toggle clasp
- chainnose and roundnose pliers
- diagonal wire cutters

SUPPLY NOTES
- All supplies for this project are available from Eclectica, (262) 641-0910.
- To make a 6½-in. (16.5cm) bracelet, use five gemstone rings. To make a 7½-in. (19.1cm) bracelet, use six rings.

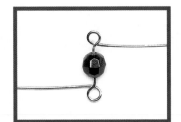

1 Cut a 2-in. (5cm) piece of wire. Make the first half of a wrapped loop (Basics, p. 12). String a round bead and make the first half of a wrapped loop parallel with the first loop. Make six or seven round-bead units.

Cut 10 to 12 ¾-in. (1.9cm) pieces of chain.

2 Attach one end of a chain to a bead unit's loop. String a gemstone ring and a metal ring on the chain. Attach the end link of the chain to the bead unit's loop. Complete the wraps.

3 Repeat step 2 on the bead unit's remaining loop. Continue attaching bead units and rings until the bracelet is within ½ in. (1.3cm) of the finished length. End with bead units, leaving the end loops unwrapped.

4 On each end loop, attach half of the clasp. Complete the wraps. ❖

Sculpt a leaf necklace & earrings

Hand shape wire into this delicate set

Shape and assemble lengths of wire to create this necklace with a simple hook-and-eye clasp. Flaunt your wireworking skills even more with a pair of earrings suspended from handmade earring wires.

by Cynthia Wuller

1 **necklace** • Determine the finished length of your necklace. (The silver necklace is 15½ in./39.4cm; the gold necklace is 16½ in./41.9cm.) Cut 18 to 24 4-in. (10cm) pieces of wire for the large leaves. Cut six 3½-in. (8.9cm) pieces for the medium leaves. Cut six 3-in. (7.6cm) pieces for the small leaves. Bend each wire in half.

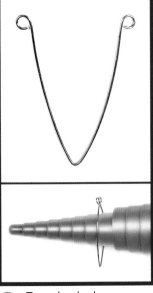

2 **a** To make the leaves: Make a loop at each end of one wire.
b Form the wire around a cylindrical object.

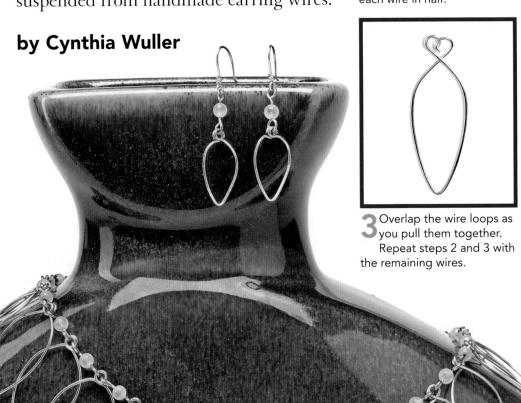

3 Overlap the wire loops as you pull them together. Repeat steps 2 and 3 with the remaining wires.

4 To make the links: Cut 30 to 35 1¾-in. (4.4cm) pieces of wire. Make a plain loop (Basics, p. 12) on one end. String a bead and make a plain loop.

EDITOR'S TIP

The Right Angle mandrel (pictured in step 2) is a useful tool for shaping wire. Visit Fiskars, fiskarscrafts.com, for more information.

5 To attach the links: Open one loop of a link (Basics). Attach the loops of a large leaf. Close the loop. Repeat with the link's remaining loop and a second large leaf.

On each end, use links to attach the remaining large leaves. Attach the medium leaves and then the small leaves.

6 To make a hook-and-eye clasp: Cut a 2½-in. (6.4cm) piece of wire. Make a plain loop on one end. Approximately ½ in. (1.3cm) from the loop, pull the wire around the largest part of your roundnose pliers.

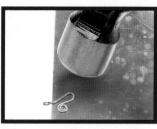

7 Form a coil on the end of the wire, and hammer the hook on a bench block or anvil.

8 Cut a 2½-in. (6.4cm) piece of wire. Make a plain loop on one end. On the other end, make a wrapped loop (Basics) large enough to accommodate the hook.

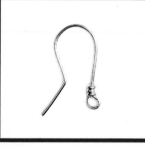

9 On each end, attach half of the clasp to the loops of a leaf.

1 **earrings •** Cut a 3-in. (7.6cm) piece of wire. Bend the wire in half. Follow steps 2 and 3 of the necklace to make a small leaf.

Cut a 1¾-in. (4.4cm) piece of wire. Make a link as in step 4 of the necklace. Open a loop of the link (Basics, p. 12) and attach the loops of the leaf. Close the loop.

Repeat to make a second dangle.

2 Cut two 3-in. (7.6cm) pieces of wire. Make a bend ¼ in. (6mm) from one end of each wire. Pull the wires around a cylindrical object ½ in. (1.3cm) from the bend.

3 On one end of each wire, make a single wrapped loop (Basics).

4 Open the loop of a dangle and attach an earring wire. Close the loop. Repeat with the second dangle. ❖

Supply List

necklace
- 16-in. (41cm) strand 4–5mm beads
- 14–17 ft. (4.3–5.2m) 20-gauge half-hard wire
- chainnose and roundnose pliers
- diagonal wire cutters
- bench block or anvil
- hammer
- mandrel

earrings
- **2** 4–5mm beads
- 16 in. (41cm) 20-gauge half-hard wire
- chainnose and roundnose pliers
- diagonal wire cutters
- mandrel

Clasp

Preserve a treasure in a trendy pendant

Pocket-wat

by Jane Konkel

Lockets are making another comeback. So you can get a little sentimental when you choose a photo, mementos, or tiny trinkets to encase in this glass-front pendant. Bird beads and filigree drops make a romantic pair of earrings.

1 necklace • Use a coin to remove the back of a pocket-watch pendant. Cut out a 20mm round picture. Make sure the picture is right side up and centered, and glue it to the inside of the watch back.

2 Cut a 2½-in. (6.4cm) piece of wire. Make the first half of a wrapped loop (Basics, p. 12). Attach a charm and complete the wraps. String one or two 3–4mm beads and the hole of the pendant. Make a wrapped loop.

EDITOR'S TIP
If you prefer a more colorful necklace, substitute a beaded strand for one of the chains. And use one or two beads in the earrings as well. A 4mm bicone crystal nestles nicely between each bird's wings.

3 If desired, place a few watch parts inside the pendant. Reattach the back of the pendant.

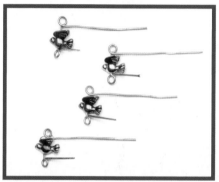

4 Trim the head from a head pin. Make the first half of a wrapped loop. String a bird bead and make the first half of a wrapped loop. Make four bead units.

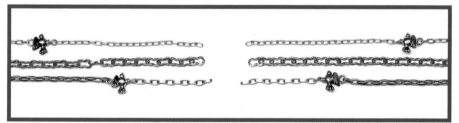

5 Decide how long you want your necklace to be. (My necklace is 23 in./58cm.) Cut three pieces of chain to that length. Cut each chain in half.
   Cut one chain 2½ in. (6.4cm) from one end. Attach a loop of a bead unit to each end, and complete the wraps. Repeat with the remaining half of the chain.
   Cut another chain 1½ in. (3.8cm) from one end. Attach a loop of a bead unit to each end, and complete the wraps. Repeat with the remaining half of the chain.

ch locket

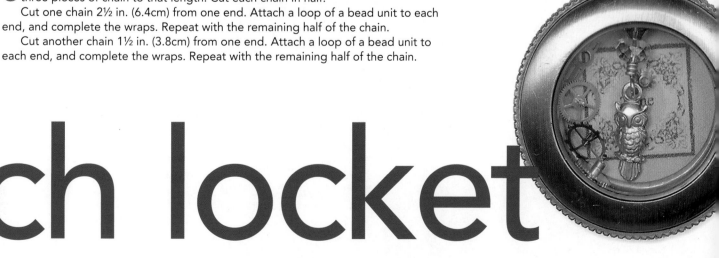

6 Make two bead units as in step 4. Attach one loop of each to the pendant and the remaining loop to three chains. Complete the wraps.

7 On each end, open a jump ring (Basics) and attach a chain and the corresponding loop of half of a clasp. Close the jump ring. Repeat to attach each remaining chain.

1 earrings • Trim the head from a head pin. Make the first half of a wrapped loop (Basics, p. 12). Attach a filigree drop and complete the wraps.

Supply List

All supplies from Ornamentea, (919) 834-6260, ornamentea.com.

necklace
• 30mm pocket-watch pendant
• 20mm round picture
• **6** 10mm bird beads, in different finishes
• 4–8mm flat charm
• **1–2** 3–4mm beads
• **3–7** 2–5mm watch parts or other trinkets (optional)
• 2½ in. (6.4cm) 24-gauge half-hard wire

• 4–5 ft. (1.2–1.5m) chain, in three styles
• **6** 3-in. (7.6cm) head pins
• **6** 5mm jump rings
• three-strand toggle clasp
• chainnose and roundnose pliers
• diagonal wire cutters
• Dazzle-Tac glue

earrings
• **2** 20mm filigree drops
• **2** 10mm bird beads
• 1 in. (2.5cm) chain, 2–3mm links
• **2** 3-in. (7.6cm) head pins
• pair of earring wires
• chainnose and roundnose pliers
• diagonal wire cutters

2 String a bird bead and make the first half of a wrapped loop perpendicular to the first loop. Cut a ½-in. (1.3cm) piece of chain. Attach the loop and complete the wraps.

3 Open the loop of an earring wire (Basics). Attach the dangle and close the loop. Make a second earring to match the first. ✦

Sparkling rings

Wrap a ring of wire and crystals

by Mia Gofar

With a few twists and turns, you can make a simple, pretty crystal ring. Since each one takes only a few minutes, make several for yourself and some to give away, too.

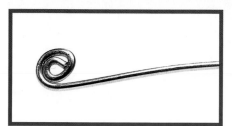

1 Cut a 12–13-in. (30–33cm) piece of wire. Grasp the end of the wire with the tip of your roundnose pliers and form a small loop. After a complete turn, grasp the wire with chainnose pliers. Continue to form a spiral with your fingers until you have two or three coils.

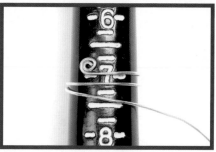

2 Place the coil against a ring mandrel at a slightly smaller ring size than desired. Wrap the wire tightly around the mandrel twice, leaving approximately ⅛ in. (3mm) between wraps.

3 Bend the wire upward. Make a horizontal bend ⅛ in. (3mm) from the previous bend, as shown.
String three crystals flush with the last bend. Make two bends next to the last crystal as shown.

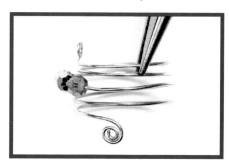

4 Wrap the wire twice around the mandrel. Remove the ring, and make a spiral on the end of the wire. Trim the excess wire. ✤

Supply List

- **3** 4mm crystals
- 12–13 in. (30–33cm) 22-gauge craft wire
- chainnose and roundnose pliers
- diagonal wire cutters
- ring mandrel (Auntie's Beads, auntiesbeads.com)

EDITOR'S TIP
Use 22-gauge craft wire for the rings. It is malleable but still holds its shape.

Angular chain balances gemstones in
a necklace-and-earring set

by Brenda Schweder

Create
an elegant drape
with beads and chain

For a unified design, select rectangular gemstones that have a rich
pattern. Then, find chains that accentuate the pattern. Figaro or curb
chains, with their angular links, also complement the beads' shapes.

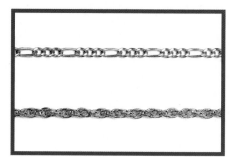

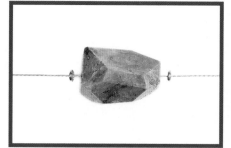

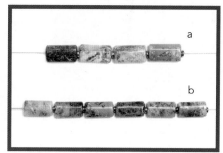

1 necklace • For the shortest strand:
Determine the finished length of
your necklace. Subtract 1 in. (2.5cm) and
cut a piece of 6–8mm-link chain
to that length. (My shortest strands
are 14½ in./36.8cm.) For the middle
strand, cut a piece of 4–5mm-link
chain 1½–2 in. (3.8–5cm) longer than the
previous piece.

2 For the longest strand, cut a 15-in.
(38cm) piece of beading wire. String
a spacer, an accent bead, and a spacer.

> **EDITOR'S TIP**
> Consider using vintage or
> base-metal chain, both of which
> have patinas that echo darker
> gemstone patterns.

3 a On one end, string an alternating
pattern of four rectangular beads
and four spacers.
  b On the other end, string an
alternating pattern of six rectangular
beads and six spacers.

4 Cut two 5–7-in. (13–18cm) pieces of 4–5mm-link chain.

On each end of the wire, string a crimp bead and one chain. Go back through the last few beads strung and tighten the wire. Crimp the crimp bead (Basics, p. 12) and trim the excess wire.

5 Using chainnose pliers, close a crimp cover over each crimp bead.

6 Check the fit, allowing 1 in. (2.5cm) for finishing. Trim chain, if necessary. On each end, open a 4–5mm jump ring (Basics). Attach one end of each chain and a soldered jump ring. Close the jump ring.

On one end, attach an S-hook clasp. Close half of the S with chainnose pliers.

1 earrings • On a decorative head pin, string a rectangular bead. Make a plain or wrapped loop (Basics, p. 12).

2 Cut a 1½-in. (3.8cm) piece of 4–5mm-link chain and a 1¾-in. (4.4cm) piece of 6–8mm-link chain. Open the loop of an earring wire (Basics). Attach the bead unit and each chain. Close the loop. Make a second earring to match the first. ❖

SupplyList

necklace
- 24–30mm accent bead
- 16-in. (41cm) strand rectangular beads, approximately 8 x 16mm
- **12** 3–4mm flat spacers
- flexible beading wire, .014 or .015
- 14–17 in. (36–43cm) chain, 6–8mm links
- 24–32 in. (61–81cm) chain, 4–5mm links
- **2** 4–5mm jump rings
- **2** crimp beads
- **2** crimp covers
- S-hook clasp with **2** soldered jump rings
- chainnose pliers
- diagonal wire cutters
- crimping pliers (optional)

earrings
- **2** rectangular beads, approximately 8 x 16mm, left over from necklace
- 4 in. (10cm) chain, 6–8mm links
- 3½ in. (8.9cm) chain, 4–5mm links
- **2** 2-in. (5cm) decorative head pins
- pair of earring wires
- chainnose and roundnose pliers
- diagonal wire cutters

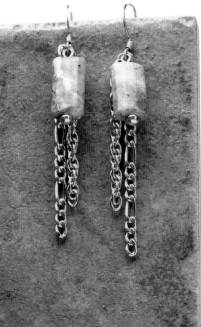

Singularly stylish earrings

Try a one-sided take on bead caps

by Sara Strauss

Bead caps are typically strung on each side of a round bead. Try an unconventional design by stringing an oversized bead cap on just one side of a flat bead. Suspend the dangle from fine chain for a stylish design.

1 On a head pin, string a bead cap and a flat bead. Make a plain loop (Basics, p. 12).

2 Cut a ¾-in. (1.9cm) piece of chain. Open the loop of the bead unit (Basics) and attach the chain. Close the loop.

3 Open the loop of an earring wire (Basics). Attach the dangle and close the loop. Make a second earring to match the first. ✤

SupplyList

- **2** 8–12mm flat beads
- **2** 8–12mm bead caps
- **1½ in. (3.8cm) chain, 2–3mm links
- **2** 1½-in. (3.8cm) head pins
- pair of earring wires
- chainnose and roundnose pliers
- diagonal wire cutters

DESIGN GUIDELINE

For dramatic earrings, use longer chain with 4–5mm links, 12–18mm beads, and 12–18mm bead caps.

Make a
CONNECTION

Hook up a stylish bracelet and earrings by linking jump rings

Use jump rings to make a chain that balances the size of the beads in these bracelets. Select precision-cut jump rings, which have flush-cut ends that align evenly when you close them. Since you'll be opening and closing many jump rings, make sure you have a second pair of chainnose pliers.

by Robyn Rosen

1 bracelet • Cut a 7-in. (18cm) piece of wire. Center: accent bead, bead cap, focal bead, bead cap, accent bead.

DESIGN GUIDELINE
Make a mixed-metal bracelet by combining copper-colored beads with silver spacers and jump rings.

2 Decide how long you want your bracelet to be. String an alternating pattern of spacers and metal beads on each end until the beaded section is half the finished length of your bracelet. Make the first half of a wrapped loop (Basics, p. 12).

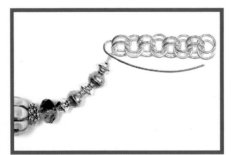

4 Attach a jump ring section to each loop of the beaded section. Complete the wraps.

3 Open two jump rings (Basics). Attach two jump rings to the first two as shown. Close the jump rings. Continue attaching pairs of jump rings until the jump ring section is about 1½ in. (3.8cm) long. Repeat to make a second jump ring section.

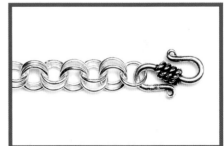

5 Check the fit, allowing 1 in. (2.5cm) for finishing. Add or remove pairs of jump rings from each end, if necessary. On one end, use a jump ring to attach a hook or S-hook clasp. On the other end, attach four or five connected single jump rings.

SupplyList

bracelet
- 12–16mm focal bead
- **2** 8–10mm accent beads
- **4–6** 5–7mm metal beads
- **6–8** 4–6mm spacers
- **2** 8–13mm bead caps
- 7 in. (18cm) 18- or 20-gauge half-hard wire
- **25–50** 4–5mm 18-gauge jump rings (Urban Maille Chain Works, urbanmaille.com)
- hook or S-hook clasp
- 2 pairs of chainnose pliers
- roundnose pliers
- diagonal wire cutters

earrings
- **2** 12–16mm beads
- **2** 4mm bicone crystals
- **2** 8–13mm bead caps
- **2** 1½-in. (3.8cm) head pins
- **2** 4–5mm 18-gauge jump rings (Urban Maille Chain Works, urbanmaille.com)
- pair of earring wires
- chainnose and roundnose pliers
- diagonal wire cutters

1 earrings • On a head pin, string a bicone crystal, a 12–16mm bead, and a bead cap. Make a plain loop (Basics, p. 12).

2 Open a jump ring (Basics). Attach the dangle and an earring wire. Close the jump ring. Make a second earring to match the first. ✤

Go
by Rupa Balachandar

bohemian

Jeweled earrings make for fast fashion

Big earrings are one of the season's key pieces of jewelry. Go bold with filigrees decorated with brilliant crystals, including some easy-to-attach flat-back crystals. Changing the type of chain or size of crystals will create a whole new look for these free-spirited earrings.

1. Glue flat-back crystals to a filigree finding as shown, attaching nine flat backs of one color and eight of a second color. Allow to dry overnight.

2. On a head pin, string a 3mm bicone crystal, a 4mm bicone crystal, and a 3mm bicone. Make a plain loop (Basics, p. 12). Make nine bead units.

3. Open the loop (Basics) of a bead unit. Attach the center loop of the filigree finding. Close the loop. Attach the remaining bead units to the filigree's loops, leaving the outer loops open.

SupplyList

- 2 50mm filigree findings with 11 loops
- 18 4mm bicone crystals
- 36 3mm bicone crystals
- 34 3mm flat-back crystals, 18 in one color and 16 in a second color
- 7 in. (18cm) chain, 4–5mm links
- 18 1-in. (2.5cm) head pins
- 6 4–5mm jump rings
- pair of lever-back earring wires
- chainnose and roundnose pliers
- diagonal wire cutters
- Gem-Tac or Aleene's Platinum Bond Glass & Bead adhesive (Michaels, michaels.com for store locations)

4. Cut two 1½-in. (3.8cm) pieces of chain. Open a jump ring (Basics) and attach a chain to an outer loop of the filigree. Close the jump ring. Use a jump ring to attach the second chain.

EDITOR'S TIP
When gluing, hold each flat-back crystal with chainnose pliers to help you position it on a filigree finding.

5. Use a jump ring to attach both chains to an earring wire. Make a second earring to match the first. ❖

One good turn...

Curves and coils connect in a custom necklace

Form this wire necklace with three easy coiling techniques. With a few turns of your roundnose pliers, you can make double coils, figure-eight links, and a hook clasp. Then, connect these ornamental components for a shapely piece.

by Paloma Ramos-Tapia

Supply List

- **3** 20mm beads
- 7–9 ft. (2.1–2.7m) 18-gauge half-hard wire
- chainnose, nylon-jaw, and roundnose pliers
- diagonal wire cutters
- metal file or emery board

1 To make a bead unit: Cut a 5-in. (13cm) piece of wire. On one end, use the tip of your roundnose pliers to make a loop. Form a coil around the loop. String a bead, and make a coil in the opposite direction. Make three bead units.

2 To make a double-coil link: Cut a 4-in. (10cm) piece of wire. On each end, use the tip of your roundnose pliers to make a loop, and form coils in opposite directions. Leave ¼ in. (6mm) of wire uncoiled between the coils. Make 11 to 15 double-coil links.

EDITOR'S TIP

When you're forming a coil, use the tip of your roundnose pliers to make the initial loop. Then, grasp the loop with nylon-jaw pliers, and form the rest of the coil by pulling the wire around the loop with your fingers. Reposition the nylon-jaw pliers as necessary to form a tight coil.

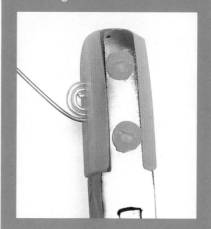

3 To make a figure-eight link: Cut a 1¼-in. (3.2cm) piece of wire. On one end, use the largest part of your roundnose pliers to make a loop. Make a loop on the remaining end, in the opposite direction. Make 14 to 18 figure-eight links.

4 To make a hook clasp: Cut an 8-in. (20cm) piece of wire. Make a small loop at one end. Place your roundnose pliers next to the loop, and bring the wire around the jaw of the pliers.

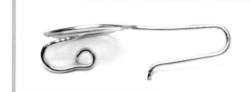

5 Wrap the wire around the tip of your roundnose pliers, forming a coil approximately ½ in. (1.3cm) in diameter.

Approximately ½ in. (1.3cm) from the coil, make a hook by pulling the wire around the largest part of your roundnose pliers. Make a small bend at the end. Trim the excess wire and file the end.

6 Open a loop (Basics, p. 12) of a figure-eight link and attach a coil of a bead unit. Close the loop.

7 Attach another bead unit's coil to the remaining loop of the figure-eight link.

Use a figure-eight link to attach the remaining bead unit.

8 On each end, attach an alternating pattern of figure-eight and double-coil links until the necklace is within 1 in. (2.5cm) of the finished length. (The silver necklace is 16 in./41cm; the gold necklace is 18½ in./47cm.) End with a double-coil link.

9 On one end, use a figure-eight link to attach the hook clasp. ❖

Quick coiled bracelet

Flower beads bloom among
wire butterflies

by Jean Yates

Make spirals to resemble butterfly wings
with this simple wire technique. Use
beads or coils of various sizes to produce a
number of different compositions that
showcase distinctive art beads.

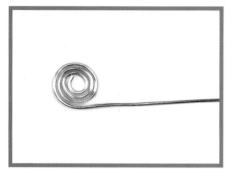

1 Cut a 6-in. (15cm) piece of wire. Using roundnose pliers, make a loop on one end. Coil the wire around the loop three or four times to make a 10mm coil. (See tip on p. 109.)

2 String a bead on the wire, and coil the remaining end of the wire toward the bead.

3 Repeat steps 1 and 2 with the same bead. Make five bead units.

4 Open a 10mm jump ring (Basics, p. 12). Attach a bead unit's coil and one coil of another bead unit. Close the jump ring. Attach the remaining coils below and on the other side of the beads. Repeat, connecting the remaining bead units.

5 Cut four pieces of chain, each approximately ½ in. (1.3cm). Use a 9mm jump ring to attach a chain and an end coil. Repeat with each remaining chain and end coil.

6 On each end, use a 9mm jump ring to attach each pair of chains and half a toggle clasp. ❖

Supply List

- **5** lampworked beads, approximately 15mm (black beads by Kim Miles, kimmiles.com; white beads by Bindy Lambell, bindy.com)
- **5** ft. (1.5m) 20-gauge half-hard wire
- **2–4** in. (5–10cm) chain, 4–6mm links
- **8** 10mm 16-gauge jump rings (Fire Mountain Gems, 800-355-2137, firemountaingems.com)
- **6** 9mm 16-gauge jump rings
- toggle clasp
- chainnose and roundnose pliers
- diagonal wire cutters
- nylon-jaw pliers (optional)

Rosy glow

Wire flourishes make
a necklace-and-
earring set shine

by Mia Gofar

This necklace starts with soft suede,
but rosy crystals cradled in gleaming
wire make it truly radiant. Although
you can make loops with roundnose
pliers, this would be an excellent
opportunity to try your hand at
using a wire jig.

1 necklace • Cut a 4-in.
(10cm) piece of wire.
Make a plain loop (Basics,
p. 12) at one end and string a
diamond-shaped bead.

2 Make a wrapped loop
(Basics) above the bead,
but don't trim the excess wire.
Wrap the excess wire around
the bead and make one wrap
next to the plain loop.
   Make a total of three
diamond-shaped units and
one round-crystal unit.

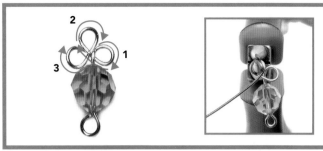

3 Cut a 4-in. (10cm) piece of wire. Make a plain loop at one end and string a crystal. Using roundnose pliers or a wire jig, make a three-loop clover as shown. Trim the excess wire.

4 Open a jump ring (Basics) and attach one loop of the crystal unit from step 2 and a diamond-shaped unit. Close the jump ring.

Open the single loop (Basics) of the three-loop clover and attach the remaining loop of the diamond-shaped unit. Close the loop.

5 Decide how long you want your necklace to be. (My necklaces are 19 in./48cm.) Subtract 5 in. (13cm) and cut a piece of suede cord to that length. Cut the cord in half. On one end of each piece, attach a crimp end (Basics).

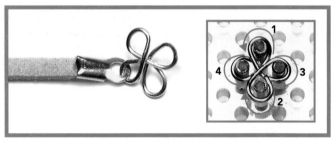

6 Cut a 4-in. (10cm) piece of wire. Using roundnose pliers or a wire jig, make a four-loop clover as shown. Trim the excess wire. Attach one loop to one of the crimp ends. Repeat.

7 Cut a 3-in. (7.6cm) piece of wire. Make the first half of a wrapped loop on one end. String a crystal and make the first half of a wrapped loop. Attach one loop to a four-loop clover. Attach the other loop to a wrapped loop of a diamond-shaped unit. Complete the wraps. Repeat on the other end.

8 Attach one loop of the three-loop clover to the remaining loop of a diamond-shaped unit. Repeat.

9 Check the fit, allowing 1 in. (2.5cm) for the clasp. Trim cord from each end, if necessary. Attach a crimp end to each cord end.

On one end, use a jump ring to attach a lobster claw clasp and a crimp end. Repeat on the other end, substituting a soldered jump ring for the clasp.

SupplyList

necklace
- **3** diamond-shaped beads, approximately 10 x 15mm
- **4** 8mm round crystals
- **12–16** in. (30–41cm) suede cord
- **34** in. (86cm) 20-gauge half-hard wire
- **3** 4–5mm jump rings
- **4** crimp ends
- lobster claw clasp and

- soldered jump ring
- chainnose and roundnose pliers
- diagonal wire cutters
- wire jig (optional)

earrings
- **2** 10–12mm round crystals
- **8** in. (20cm) 20-gauge half-hard wire
- pair of earring wires
- chainnose and roundnose pliers
- diagonal wire cutters

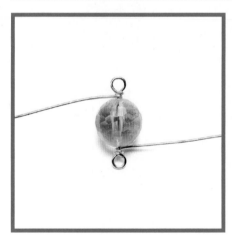

1 earrings • Cut a 4-in. (10cm) piece of wire. Make a wrapped loop (Basics, p. 12) on one end. Do not trim the excess wire. String a crystal and make a wrapped loop, leaving the excess wire.

2 Using roundnose pliers, bend each remaining wire into a coil on one side of the crystal. Trim the excess wire.

3 Open the loop of an earring wire (Basics). Attach the dangle. Close the loop. Make a second earring to match the first. ❖

Different charm sizes make for balanced earrings • by Brenda Schweder

Combine charms in mixed-metal earrings

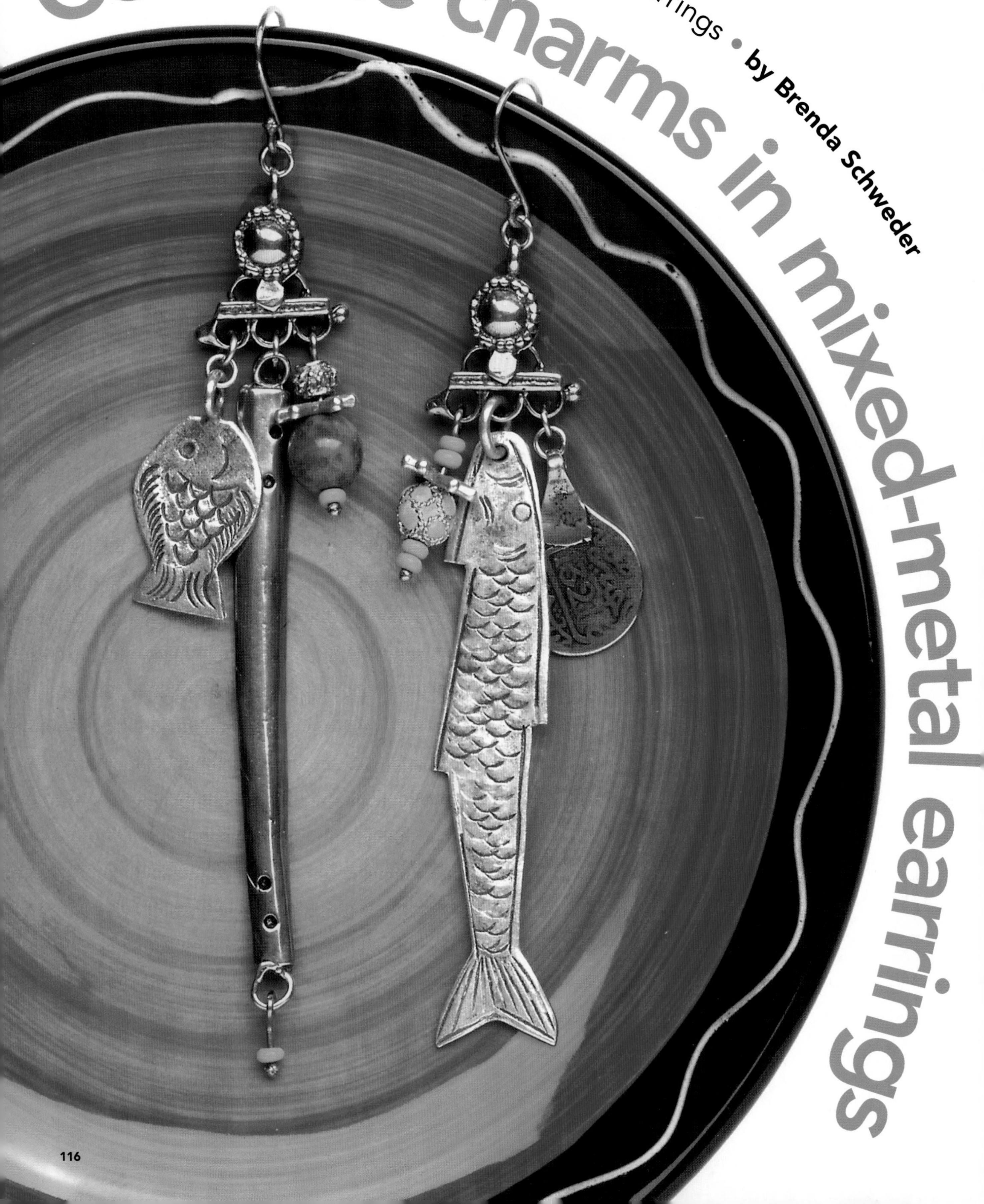

With mismatched earrings, you won't have to fish around for a fun accessory. The key to these earrings is proportion; the weight of each earring balances the other. A bit of aqua adds color and keeps them bright and cheerful.

1 To make the first earring: On a decorative head pin, string a 3mm bead. Make a 5mm plain loop (Basics, p. 12). On another decorative head pin, string a 3mm bead, an 8mm bead, a flat spacer, and a 5mm spacer. Make a 5mm plain loop.

2 Open the loop of the smaller bead unit (Basics). Attach the loop of the narrow end of a tapered bar. Close the loop.

Open a 4mm jump ring (Basics). Attach the tapered bar to a connector's center loop. Close the jump ring.

3 Use two 4mm jump rings to attach a small fish charm to an outer loop of the connector. Attach the larger bead unit's loop to the remaining outer loop.

4 To make the second earring: On a decorative head pin, string two 3mm beads, a 6mm bead, a flat spacer, and two 3mm beads. Make a 5mm plain loop.

5 Use a 5–6mm jump ring to attach a large fish charm to a connector's center loop. Use two 4mm jump rings to attach a coin to an outer loop of the connector. Attach the bead unit's loop to the remaining outer loop.

6 Use a 4mm jump ring to attach each dangle to the loop of an earring wire. ❖

Supply List

- 6 x 65mm tapered bar with loops
- 12 x 60mm fish charm
- 14 x 25mm fish charm
- 14mm coin with loop
- 8mm round bead
- 6mm round bead
- 6 3mm beads
- 2 8mm flat spacers
- 5mm spacer

- 2 18mm three-to-one connector bars
- 3 1½-in. (3.8cm) decorative head pins
- 5–6mm jump ring
- 7 4mm jump rings
- pair of earring wires
- chainnose and roundnose pliers
- diagonal wire cutters

EDITOR'S TIP
Whether you choose silver or gold, use head pins, connectors, and earring wires in the same color to unify the design.

Tiny works of art

Silver frames showcase favorite beads in versatile earrings

by Sue Godfrey

Spend ten minutes to make something that will be appreciated forever. These simple earrings can capture the personality of a multitude of wearers depending on the combination of beads and frame you choose.

SUPPLY NOTE

The frames are available from many places, including Midwest Beads, midwestbeads.com, and Auntie's Beads, auntiesbeads.com.

Supply List

- **2** 15–20mm open-center frame beads
- **6–12** 2–8mm beads and spacers
- **2** 2½-in. (6.4cm) head pins
- pair of earring wires
- chainnose and roundnose pliers
- diagonal wire cutters

EDITOR'S TIPS

- Shake things up by stringing different beads in matching frames. Or, string the same set of beads in a different order in each earring.
- If the bottom hole of the frame is larger than the head of a head pin, string a seed bead or spacer on the head pin before step 1.

1 On a head pin, string the bottom hole of a frame, several beads, and the top hole of the frame.

2 Make a wrapped loop (Basics, p. 12).

3 Open the loop of an earring wire (Basics). Attach the dangle. Close the loop. Make a second earring to match the first. ❖

Shortcuts

Readers' tips to make your beading life easier

1 visual aids
There are no bead shops where I live, so I buy beads online. Visualizing projects is sometimes difficult because I don't have the beads in front of me. To make shopping easier, I create a desktop folder and put the pictures of all my favorite things from a Web site in it. I use the computer's thumbnails feature to look at all my potential purchases side by side.
– *Chantal Edwards, via e-mail*

2 power cleaning
Thrift-store beads sometimes require a more thorough cleaning than just a swipe of a cloth. An old electric toothbrush and a drop of dish soap in warm water will usually do the job.
– *Karen Fox, Broken Arrow, Okla.*

3 instant scoops
A sticky note folded adhesive-to-adhesive will serve as a pliable, inexpensive, and disposable scoop for tiny beads.
– *Linda Paul, Shorewood, Wis.*

4 recycling wire
I use small pieces of leftover wire to make small charms, jump rings, and clasps. If the wire has nicks, I hammer it flat to hide the flaws and create an artistic look. This way, I have custom-made, inexpensive findings.
– *Mollie Chen, Bloomington, Ind.*

5 quick clean up
An adhesive lint roller will quickly pick up seed beads, crimp beads, and tiny wire bits from your work surface. You can remove anything you want to keep and throw the rest away.
– *Marie Rankin, Ontario, Canada*

Gemstones

Pear-shaped
gemstones anchor
a lavish necklace,
bracelet, and earrings

by Lori Anderson

Multiple elements used in these pieces
offer an opportunity to play with color
combinations. Try an unexpected
arrangement — like copper, turquoise, and
tourmalinated quartz — or stick with one
color family for a more classic look.

String these
EYE-CATCHING
GEMS

1 **necklace** • Cut a 3-in. (7.6cm) piece of 24-gauge wire. String a pear-shaped bead and make a set of wraps above it (Basics, p. 12). Make the first half of a wrapped loop (Basics) above the wraps.

On a head pin, string a flat spacer, a rondelle, and a flat spacer. Make the first half of a wrapped loop. Make a total of nine rondelle units. Set one aside for step 8.

2 Cut a 1-in. (2.5cm) piece of chain. Attach eight rondelle units and the pear unit as shown. Complete the wraps.

3 **a** On a head pin, string a flat spacer, a rondelle, and a flat spacer. Make a wrapped loop. Make a total of ten rondelle units.

b On a head pin, string a 2mm spacer, a bead cap, and a 6mm round bead. Make a wrapped loop. Make a total of ten round-bead units.

c On a head pin, string a charm. Make a wrapped loop. Make a total of four charm units.

4 Cut a 17-in. (43cm) piece of beading wire. Center: two 3mm spacers, round-bead unit, rondelle unit, four 3mm spacers, rondelle unit, round-bead unit, two 3mm spacers.

5 On each end of the wire, string three pear-shaped beads.

6 On each end, string: two 3mm spacers, rondelle unit, round-bead unit, two 3mm spacers, charm unit, two 3mm spacers, rondelle unit, round-bead unit, two 3mm spacers.

Supply List

necklace

- 16-in. (41cm) strand 16mm faceted pear-shaped beads
- **19** 6mm faceted rondelles
- **10** 6mm round beads
- **4** 5–7mm charms
- **38** 4mm flat spacers
- **42** 3mm round spacers
- **10** 2mm round spacers
- **10** 6mm bead caps
- flexible beading wire, .014 or .015
- 3 in. (7.6cm) 24-gauge half-hard wire
- 12–14 in. (30–36cm) chain, 5–6mm links
- **33** 2-in. (5cm) head pins
- **2** 5–6mm jump rings
- **2** crimp beads

- lobster claw or spring-ring clasp
- chainnose and roundnose pliers
- diagonal wire cutters
- crimping pliers (optional)

bracelet

- **12** 16mm faceted pear-shaped beads, left over from necklace
- **5** 6mm faceted rondelles
- **5** 6mm round beads
- **5** 5–7mm charms
- **10** 4mm flat spacers
- **22–28** 3mm round spacers
- **5** 2mm round spacers
- **5** 6mm bead caps
- flexible beading wire, .014 or .015
- ¾ in. (1.9cm) cable chain, 5–6mm links
- **15** 2-in. (5cm) head pins
- 5–6mm jump ring
- **2** crimp beads

- toggle clasp
- chainnose and roundnose pliers
- diagonal wire cutters
- crimping pliers (optional)

earrings

- **2** 16mm faceted pear-shaped beads, left over from necklace
- **4** 6mm faceted rondelles
- **2** 6mm round beads
- **8** 4mm flat spacers
- **2** 2mm round spacers
- **2** 6mm bead caps
- 6 in. (15cm) 24-gauge half-hard wire
- 2 in. (5cm) cable chain, 5–6mm links
- **6** 2-in. (5cm) head pins
- **2** 5–6mm jump rings
- pair of earring posts with ear nuts
- chainnose and roundnose pliers
- diagonal wire cutters

7 a Repeat step 5. Repeat step 6, stringing a crimp bead between the last two spacers.

b Decide how long you want your necklace to be. (My necklaces are 17 in./43cm.) Subtract 9 in. (23cm) and cut a piece of chain to that length. Cut the chain into two pieces, cutting one piece 2 in. (5cm) longer than the other (to include a chain extender). On each end, string a piece of chain. Go back through the last few beads strung and tighten the wire. Crimp the crimp beads (Basics) and trim the excess wire. Check the fit, and trim chain from each end if necessary.

8 Open a jump ring (Basics) and attach a lobster claw clasp and the shorter piece of chain. Close the jump ring. On the other end, attach the remaining rondelle unit from step 1. Complete the wraps.

9 Use a jump ring to attach the dangle to the center of the strand.

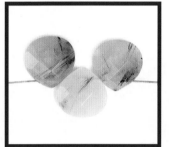

DESIGN NOTE
The necklace can be clasped anywhere along the chain, making it adjustable to a range of lengths. For additional flexibility in length, cut your chain a few inches longer, or string additional 3mm spacers on each end of the beaded strand.

1 bracelet • Follow steps 3a–3c of the necklace to make a rondelle unit, a round-bead unit, and a charm unit. Make five of each.

2 Cut a piece of beading wire (Basics, p. 12). Center: two 3mm spacers, rondelle unit, charm unit, round-bead unit, two 3mm spacers.

3 a On each end, string three pear-shaped beads.

b On each end, string the pattern in steps 2 and 3a until the bracelet is within 2 in. (5cm) of the finished length. End with bead units.

4 Cut a ¾-in. (1.9cm) piece of chain. Open a jump ring (Basics) and attach the bar half of a clasp and the chain. Close the jump ring.

On one end, string a 3mm spacer, a crimp bead, a 3mm spacer, and the chain. Repeat on the other end, substituting the loop half of the clasp for the chain. Check the fit, and add or remove beads from each end if necessary. Go back through the beads just strung and tighten the wire. Crimp the crimp beads (Basics) and trim the excess wire.

1 earrings • Follow step 1 of the necklace, making one pear-shaped unit and two rondelle units.

On a head pin, string a 2mm spacer, a bead cap, and a 6mm round bead. Make the first half of a wrapped loop. Cut a 1-in. (2.5cm) piece of chain. Attach each bead unit to the chain and complete the wraps.

2 Open a jump ring (Basics, p. 12) and attach the dangle and an earring post. Close the jump ring.

Make a second earring to match the first. ❦

Make it
YOUR
STYLE

This necklace-and-earring set's well-chosen beads show that casual doesn't mean careless

by Cathy Jakicic

The fabric and style of this tunic are casual, yet the jewel-toned floral pattern is dressier. Faceted gems and pearls are elegant, yet the simple stringing technique makes a set that's casual and easy to wear.

EDITOR'S TIP
Because much of the beading wire is visible, consider using a sterling silver or copper version.

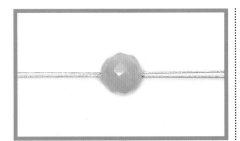

1 **necklace** • Cut two pieces of beading wire (Basics, p. 12). (My necklace is 17 in./43cm.) Center an 8mm bead over both wires.

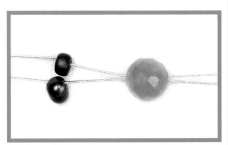

2 On each side, string a pearl on one end, a 6º seed bead on the other, and an 8mm over both ends. Repeat until the strand is within 2 in. (5cm) of the finished length.

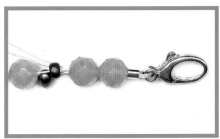

3 On one side, over both wires, string two 8mms, a crimp bead, and a lobster claw clasp. Repeat on the other side, substituting a soldered jump ring for the clasp. Check the fit, and add or remove beads from each side if necessary. Go back through the beads just strung and tighten the wires. Crimp the crimp beads (Basics) and trim the excess wire.

1 **earrings** • Cut a 5-in. (13cm) piece of beading wire. Center a pearl on the wire. String an 8mm bead over both ends.

2 String a pearl on one end and a 6º seed bead on the other. Over both ends, string an 8mm and a 6º.

3 Over both ends, string a crimp bead and the loop of an earring post. Go back through the last few beads strung and tighten the wire. Crimp the crimp bead (Basics, p. 12) and trim the excess wire. Make a second earring to match the first. ❖

SupplyList

necklace
- **26–30** 8mm faceted round beads
- **23–27** 6mm pearls, top drilled
- 1g 6º seed beads
- flexible beading wire, .014 or .015
- **2** crimp beads
- lobster claw clasp and soldered jump ring
- chainnose or crimping pliers
- diagonal wire cutters

earrings
- **4** 8mm faceted round beads
- **4** 6mm pearls, top drilled
- **4** 6º seed beads
- flexible beading wire, .014 or .015
- **2** crimp beads
- pair of earring posts with ear nuts
- chainnose or crimping pliers
- diagonal wire cutters

Rock solid

by Lindsay Hastings

Make a substantial set in no time

A fancy metal saucer surrounded by shapely quartz nuggets is this necklace's central focus. One strand of these rock-candy beads is enough to string a quick choker and a pair of matching earrings.

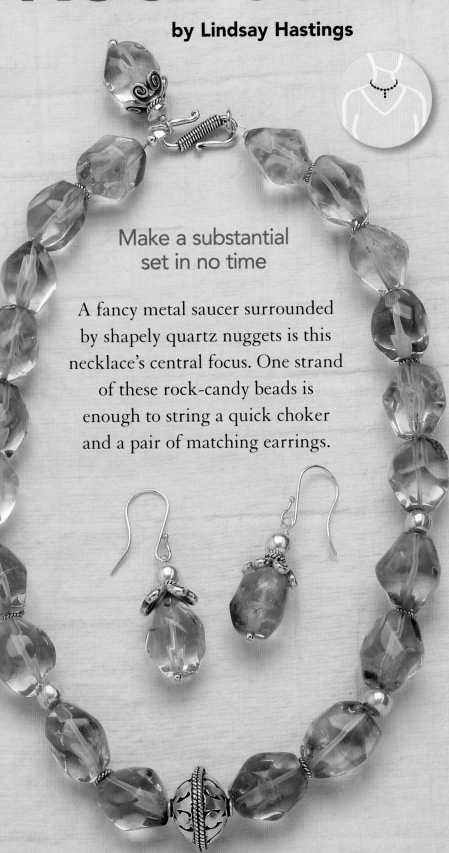

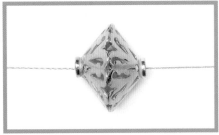

1 **necklace** • Cut a piece of beading wire (Basics, p. 12). (My necklaces are 16½ in./41.9cm.) Center a saucer bead on the wire.

2 On each end, string an 18mm bead, a 5mm spacer, an 18mm, and a 6mm barrel spacer. Repeat.

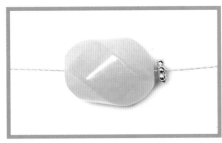

3 On each end, string an 18mm and a 5mm spacer. Repeat until the strand is within 2 in. (5cm) of the finished length. End with an 18mm.

4 On each end, string a round spacer, a crimp bead, a round spacer, and a soldered jump ring. Check the fit, and add or remove beads from each end if necessary. Go back through the last few beads strung and tighten the wire. Crimp the crimp bead (Basics) and trim the excess wire.

Attach an S-hook clasp to one jump ring. Close half of the clasp with chain-nose pliers.

5 On a head pin, string: round spacer, 18mm, bead cap, 5mm spacer, 6mm flat spacer. Make the first half of a wrapped loop (Basics). Attach the dangle to one of the jump rings and complete the wraps.

1 earrings • On a head pin, string: round spacer, 18mm bead, bead cap, 5mm spacer, 6mm barrel spacer. Make a wrapped loop (Basics, p. 12).

2 Open the loop of an earring wire (Basics). Attach the dangle and close the loop. Make a second earring to match the first. ❖

Supply List

necklace
- 18mm saucer bead
- 16-in. (41cm) strand 18mm beads
- **4** 6mm barrel spacers
- 6mm flat spacer
- **13–17** 5mm flat spacers
- **5** 3mm round spacers

- 12mm bead cap
- flexible beading wire, .014 or .015
- 2-in. (5cm) head pin
- **2** crimp beads
- S-hook clasp with **2** soldered jump rings
- chainnose and roundnose pliers
- diagonal wire cutters
- crimping pliers (optional)

earrings
- **2** 18mm beads
- **2** 6mm barrel spacers
- **2** 5mm flat spacers
- **2** 3mm round spacers
- **2** 12mm bead caps
- **2** 2-in. (5cm) head pins
- pair of earring wires
- chainnose and roundnose pliers
- diagonal wire cutters

side effects

Multicolored rondelles shine in an asymmetrical necklace and earrings • **by Rupa Balachandar**

Taking sides can be tricky, but asymmetry has its appeal. Here, mismatched rondelles — brightened with flashes of silver — converge on a contrasting pendant. Instructions are provided, but you probably won't need them. Just remember to work in small (2-in./5cm) sections so you can compare each side of the necklace as it develops.

1 **necklace** • Determine the finished length of your necklace. (My necklaces are 17½ in./ 44.5cm.) Add 6 in. (15cm) and cut a piece of beading wire to that length. Center a pendant on the wire.

On each end, string a round or bicone bead. String 1 in. (2.5cm) of rondelles and spacers in different arrangements as desired.

2 On one end, string approximately 2 in. (5cm) of assorted rondelles, accent beads, rounds, and spacers. On the other end, string 2 in. (5cm) of main-color rondelles. If desired, include spacers and an accent-color rondelle.

3 Repeat step 2 on the opposite ends of the wire.

On each end, string main-color rondelles, beads, and spacers until the necklace is within 1 in. (2.5cm) of the desired length.

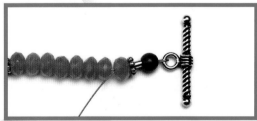

4 On each end, string a spacer, a crimp bead, a round or a bicone, and half of a clasp. Go back through the last few beads strung and tighten the wire. Check the fit, and add or remove beads from each end if necessary. Crimp the crimp beads (Basics, p. 12) and trim the excess wire.

necklace

- top-drilled pendant, approximately 30 x 40mm
- **1–2** 8–10mm accent beads
- 16-in. (41cm) strand 6mm rondelles, main color
- **10–20** 6mm rondelles, accent colors
- **4–10** 3–6mm round or bicone beads
- **10–20** 4–7mm flat spacers
- flexible beading wire, .014 or .015
- **2** crimp beads
- toggle clasp
- chainnose or crimping pliers
- diagonal wire cutters

earrings

- **2** 6mm rondelles, main color
- **2** 6mm rondelles, accent colors
- **2–4** 3–6mm flat spacers
- **2** 1½-in. (3.8cm) head pins
- pair of earring wires
- chainnose and roundnose pliers
- diagonal wire cutters

1 earrings • On a head pin, string a main-color rondelle, an accent-color rondelle, and spacers as desired. Make a plain loop (Basics, p. 12). Repeat on the other head pin with a different arrangement of rondelles and spacers, making the dangles approximately the same length.

2 Open the loop of an earring wire (Basics). Attach a dangle and close the loop. Repeat. ❖

EDITOR'S TIP

Include gemstone or shell heishi beads in your necklace. They are an economical way to add texture while maintaining the rondelle shape.

Style
with
substance

Balance a trendy, bold pendant with three chunky strands

by Carol McKinney

1 Cut a piece of beading wire (Basics, p. 12) for the shortest strand of your necklace. (The shortest strand of each of my necklaces is 16 in./41cm.) Cut two more pieces, each 2 in. (5cm) longer than the previous piece. On the longest wire, center an 8mm pearl, a pendant, and an 8mm pearl.

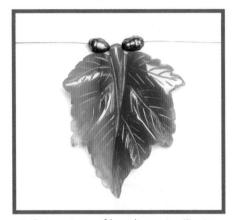

2 On each end, string beads as desired until the strand is within 2 in. (5cm) of the finished length. On the remaining wires, string beads as desired until the strands are within 2 in. (5cm) of the finished length.

3 On each end, string a spacer, a crimp bead, a spacer, and the corresponding loop of half of the clasp. Check the fit, and add or remove beads from each end if necessary. Go back through the last few beads strung and tighten the wire. Crimp the crimp beads (Basics) and trim the excess wire. ❖

Fashion forecasters see huge pendants in our future. A focal piece of this size could easily overwhelm, but not when teamed with three substantial strands. Because the pattern is unstructured, this stately necklace comes together quickly.

Supply List

- pendant, approximately 50mm
- 16-in. (41cm) strand 12mm round beads
- **2** 16-in. (41cm) strands 11mm nuggets
- **2** 16-in. (41cm) strands 10–13mm coin pearls or lentils, in two colors
- 16-in. (41cm) strand 10mm beads
- 16-in. (41cm) strand 8mm pearls
- **12** 3mm spacers
- flexible beading wire, .014 or .015
- **6** crimp beads
- three-strand clasp
- chainnose or crimping pliers
- diagonal wire cutters

EDITOR'S TIP

If your pendant is vertically drilled, make a bail. To do this, you will need 4 in. (10cm) of 20-gauge half-hard wire, chainnose pliers, and roundnose pliers. Make a plain loop (Basics, p. 12) on one end of the wire. String the pendant, and make a wrapped loop (Basics).

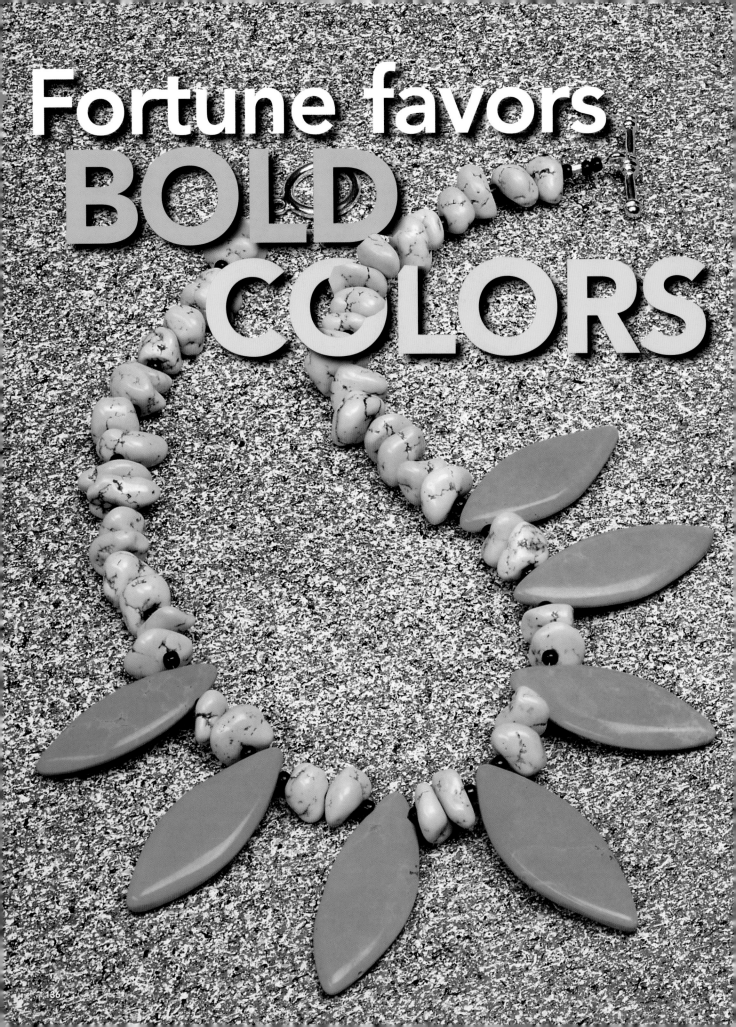

Fortune favors
BOLD COLORS

The bright gemstones in this
necklace and earrings could
attract more than admiring looks

by Andrea Loss

Australian Aborigines thought apple green gaspeite would
attract good fortune and success. Even if these cheerful
pieces don't bring you good luck, they'll give you great style.

1 **necklace** • Cut a piece
of beading wire (Basics,
p. 12). (My necklace is
17 in./43cm.)
   String: two nuggets,
8º seed bead, gaspeite
pendant, 8º, two nuggets.
Center the beads on
the wire.

2 On each end, string an 8º,
a pendant, an 8º, and two
nuggets. Repeat twice.

EDITOR'S TIP
For a bit of sparkle,
substitute 3mm crystals
for the seed beads.

3 On each end, string
an 8º and two nuggets.
Repeat until the necklace is
within 2 in. (5cm) of the
finished length.

4 On each end, string an
8º, a crimp bead, two 8ºs,
and half of a clasp. Check
the fit, and add or remove
beads from each end if
necessary. Go back through
the beads just strung and
tighten the wire. Crimp the
crimp beads (Basics) and trim
the excess wire.

1 **earrings** • On a decorative head pin, string an 8º
seed bead, two nuggets, and
an 8º. Make a wrapped loop
(Basics, p. 12).

2 Open the loop of an
earring wire (Basics) and
attach the dangle. Close the
loop. Make a second earring
to match the first. ❖

Supply**List**

necklace
- **7** 45mm marquise-cut
  gaspeite pendants,
  top drilled (Mr. Bead,
  mrbead.com)
- 16-in. (41cm) strand
  10–13mm gaspeite
  nuggets (Mr. Bead,
  mrbead.com)
- 2g 8º seed beads
- flexible beading wire,
  .018 or .019
- **2** crimp beads
- toggle clasp
- chainnose or crimping
  pliers
- diagonal wire cutters

earrings
- **4** 10–13mm gaspeite
  nuggets (Mr. Bead)
- **4** 8º seed beads
- **2** 1½-in. (3.8cm)
  decorative head pins
- pair of earring wires
- chainnose and
  roundnose pliers
- diagonal wire cutters

Glow in a spectacular necklace, bracelet, and earrings

by Eva Kapitany

For a luminous necklace, bracelet, and earring set, string this unlikely combination of shapely beads and radiant bursts of cubic zirconias. Since CZs are available in limited colors, select them first, and then choose faceted gemstones in complementary or contrasting hues.

THIS NECKLACE SHINES IN FALL COLORS

1 necklace • Cut a piece of beading wire (Basics, p. 12) for the shortest strand of your necklace. (The shortest strand of each of my necklaces is 15 in./38cm.) Cut two more, each 2 in. (5cm) longer than the previous piece.

On the shortest wire, string: cubic zirconia (CZ), ½ in. (1.3cm) of 3–4mm gemstones, three 7–9mm top-drilled beads, ½ in. (1.3cm) of 3–4mm gemstones, CZ. Center the beads.

2 On each end, string ½ in. (1.3cm) of 3–4mm gemstones, a 7–9mm bead, ½ in. (1.3cm) of 3–4mm gemstones, and a CZ. Repeat until the strand is within 2 in. (5cm) of the desired length.

3 On the middle wire, string: CZ, ¼ in. (6mm) of 3–4mm gemstones, three 10mm top-drilled beads, ¼ in. (6mm) of 3–4mm gemstones, CZ. Center the beads on the wire.

Repeat step 2 until the strand is within 2 in. (5cm) of the desired length.

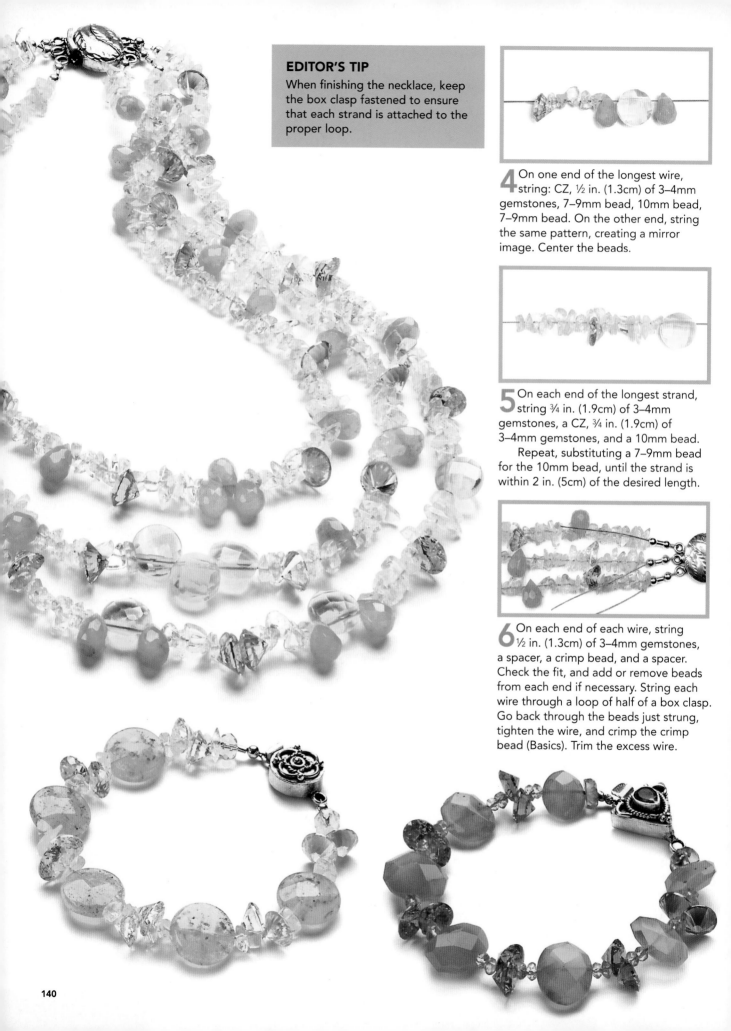

4 On one end of the longest wire, string: CZ, ½ in. (1.3cm) of 3–4mm gemstones, 7–9mm bead, 10mm bead, 7–9mm bead. On the other end, string the same pattern, creating a mirror image. Center the beads.

5 On each end of the longest strand, string ¾ in. (1.9cm) of 3–4mm gemstones, a CZ, ¾ in. (1.9cm) of 3–4mm gemstones, and a 10mm bead.
   Repeat, substituting a 7–9mm bead for the 10mm bead, until the strand is within 2 in. (5cm) of the desired length.

6 On each end of each wire, string ½ in. (1.3cm) of 3–4mm gemstones, a spacer, a crimp bead, and a spacer. Check the fit, and add or remove beads from each end if necessary. String each wire through a loop of half of a box clasp. Go back through the beads just strung, tighten the wire, and crimp the crimp bead (Basics). Trim the excess wire.

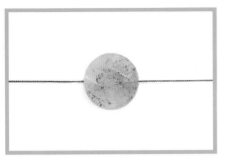

1 **bracelet** • Cut a piece of beading wire (Basics, p. 12). Center a 14mm gemstone on the wire.

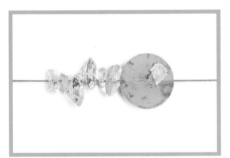

2 On each end, string: two 3–4mm gemstones, two cubic zirconias, two 3–4mm gemstones, 14mm gemstone. Repeat until the strand is within 2 in. (5cm) of the desired length.

3 On each end, string a rondelle, a crimp bead, a spacer, and half of the clasp. Check the fit, and add or remove beads from each end if necessary. Go back through the last few beads strung and tighten the wire. Crimp the crimp beads (Basics) and trim the excess wire.

SupplyList

necklace
- **7** 10mm beads, top drilled
- **26–38** 9mm cone-shaped cubic zirconias (CZs), top drilled (Better Creation Inc., 718-898-2788)
- **25–37** 7–9mm beads, top drilled
- **2** 16-in. (41cm) strands 3–4mm gemstone rondelles or chips
- **12** 3mm spacers
- flexible beading wire, .014 or .015
- **6** crimp beads
- three-strand box clasp
- chainnose or crimping pliers
- diagonal wire cutters

bracelet
- **6–8** 14mm gemstones
- **10–14** 9mm cone-shaped cubic zirconias (CZs), top drilled (Better Creation Inc., 718-898-2788)
- **2** 6mm rondelles
- **20–28** 3–4mm gemstone rondelles or chips
- **2** 3mm spacers
- flexible beading wire, .014 or .015
- **2** crimp beads
- box clasp
- chainnose or crimping pliers
- diagonal wire cutters

earrings
- **2** 14mm gemstones
- **6–10** 3–4mm gemstones
- **2** 2-in. (5cm) head pins
- pair of earring wires
- chainnose and roundnose pliers
- diagonal wire cutters

1 **earrings** • On a head pin, string a 14mm gemstone and three to five 3–4mm gemstones. Make a plain loop (Basics, p. 12).

2 Open the loop of an earring wire (Basics) and attach the dangle. Close the loop. Make a second earring to match the first. ❖

CHOOSE YOUR
POWER COLORS

Saturate a necklace, bracelet, and earrings with strong hues

by Helene Tsigistras

Match effervescent mother-of-pearl teardrops, gemstones, and seed beads to pack a powerful monochromatic punch. The design is blissfully straightforward; you can finish an impressive set in just minutes.

1 necklace • Cut a piece of beading wire (Basics, p. 12). (My necklaces are 20 in./51cm.) Center a 16mm bead on the wire.

2 On each end, string an 8º seed bead, a teardrop bead, an 8º, and a 16mm. Repeat until the strand is within 1 in. (2.5cm) of the finished length.

3 On each end, string an 8º, a crimp bead, an 8º, and half a clasp. Check the fit, and add or remove beads from each end if necessary. Go back through the last few beads strung and tighten the wire. Crimp the crimp bead (Basics) and trim the excess wire.

bracelet • Cut a piece of beading wire (Basics, p. 12). String an 8º seed bead, a teardrop bead, an 8º, and a 16mm bead. Repeat until the strand is within 1 in. (2.5cm) of the finished length. Finish as in step 3 of the necklace.

SupplyList

necklace
- 16-in. (41cm) strand 16mm gemstone beads
- 16-in. (41cm) strand 15mm mother-of-pearl teardrop beads
- 2g 8º seed beads
- flexible beading wire, .014 or .015
- **2** crimp beads
- toggle clasp
- chainnose or crimping pliers
- diagonal wire cutters

bracelet
- **5–7** 16mm gemstone beads
- **5–7** 15mm mother-of-pearl teardrop beads
- 1g 8º seed beads
- flexible beading wire, .014 or .015
- **2** crimp beads
- toggle clasp
- chainnose or crimping pliers
- diagonal wire cutters

earrings
- **2** 15mm mother-of-pearl teardrop beads
- 6 in. (15cm) 24-gauge half-hard wire
- 2¼ in. (5.7cm) chain, 2–3mm links
- pair of earring wires
- chainnose and roundnose pliers
- diagonal wire cutters

1 earrings • Cut a 3-in. (7.6cm) piece of wire. String a teardrop bead and make a set of wraps above it (Basics, p. 12). Make the first half of a wrapped loop (Basics) above the wraps.

2 Cut a 1-in. (2.5cm) piece of chain. Attach the loop to the chain and complete the wraps.

3 Open the loop of an earring wire (Basics) and attach the dangle. Close the loop. Make a second earring to match the first. ❖

EDITOR'S TIP
Because mother-of-pearl teardrop beads are available in limited colors, choose those first. Then choose a gemstone strand to match the color.

EASY LOOPS
connect stylish chain and stunning
BRIOLETTES

The right chain makes an eye-catching necklace and earrings easy

by Marla Gulotta

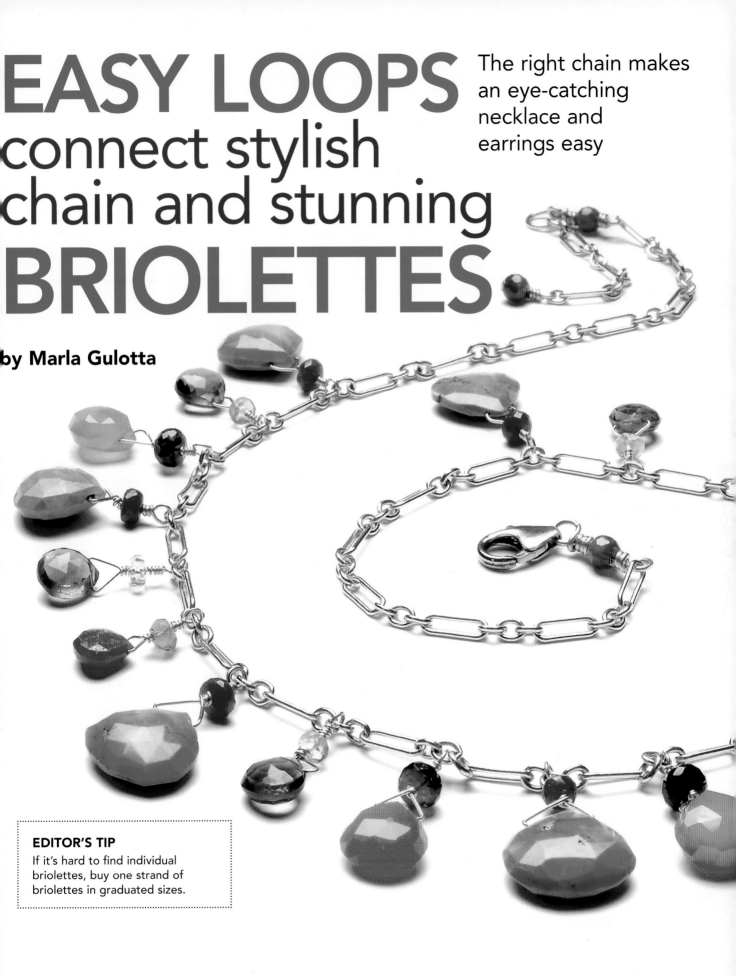

EDITOR'S TIP
If it's hard to find individual briolettes, buy one strand of briolettes in graduated sizes.

Suspend briolettes and faceted rondelles from long-and-short-link chain. Thanks to the chain's symmetry, attaching the colorful dangles is simple because there's no measuring or counting links. Two short pieces of leftover chain are just right for graceful earrings.

1 **necklace** • Cut a 3-in. (7.6cm) piece of 26-gauge wire. String a 13–15mm (large) briolette and make a set of wraps (Basics, p. 12). String a 6mm rondelle and make the first half of a wrapped loop (Basics) perpendicular to the briolette. Make a total of 17 to 19 units: nine to 11 large units and eight small units, using 4mm rondelles.

2 Decide how long you want your necklace to be. (The silver necklace is 20½ in./52.1cm; the gold necklace, 21½ in./54.6cm.) Cut a piece of chain to that length. Cut a 2-in. (5cm) piece of chain for the extender and set it aside for step 5.

Attach a large-briolette unit to the long chain's center link and complete the wraps.

3 On each side of the center unit, attach the following bead units to subsequent short links: large-briolette unit, small-briolette unit, large, small, small.

Repeat until the last bead unit is within 8 in. (20cm) of the finished length. Check the fit, allowing 1½ in. (3.8cm) for finishing, and trim chain from each end if necessary.

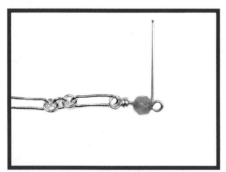

4 Cut a 2½-in. (6.4cm) piece of 22-gauge wire. Make the first half of a wrapped loop. Repeat.

On each end, attach a loop and complete the wraps. String a round bead and make the first half of a wrapped loop.

5 On one end, attach a lobster claw clasp and complete the wraps.

On the other end, attach a soldered jump ring and complete the wraps. Open a jump ring (Basics). Attach the soldered jump ring and the chain extender. Close the jump ring.

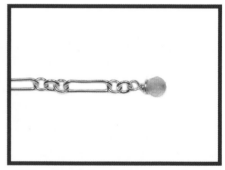

6 On a head pin, string a round bead and make the first half of a wrapped loop. Attach the bead unit to the chain and complete the wraps.

1 earrings • Make a large-briolette unit as in step 1 of the necklace, omitting the rondelle. Cut a piece of chain consisting of a long link and two short links. Attach the briolette unit to the long link and complete the wraps.

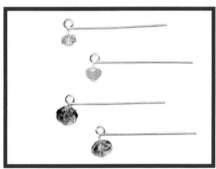

2 On a head pin, string a 4mm rondelle and make the first half of a wrapped loop (Basics, p. 12). Make a total of four rondelle units: two 4mm units and two 6mm units.

3 Attach each 6mm unit to the top link. Attach each 4mm unit to the middle link. Complete the wraps.

4 Open the loop of an earring wire (Basics). Attach the dangle and close the loop. Make a second earring to match the first. ❖

SupplyList

necklace
- **9–11** 13–15mm briolettes, in two colors
- **8** 7–9mm briolettes, in two colors
- **9–11** 6mm rondelles, in two colors
- **8** 4mm rondelles, in two colors
- **3** 4mm round beads
- **51–57** in. (1.3–1.4m) 26-gauge half-hard wire
- **5** in. (13cm) 22-gauge half-hard wire
- **19–24** in. (48–61cm) long-and-short-link chain (JewelrySupply.com, 916-780-9610)
- 1½-in. (3.8cm) head pin
- 4–5mm jump ring
- lobster claw clasp and 4–5mm soldered jump ring
- chainnose and roundnose pliers
- diagonal wire cutters

earrings
- **2** 13–15mm briolettes
- **4** 6mm rondelles, in two colors
- **4** 4mm rondelles, in two colors
- **6** in. (15cm) 26-gauge half-hard wire
- 1½ in. (3.8cm) long-and-short-link chain
- **8** 1½-in. (3.8cm) head pins
- pair of earring wires
- chainnose and roundnose pliers
- diagonal wire cutters

A clever clasp gives simple strands four variations

Twist2necklaces

by Deb Huber

String two long individual strands and use a twister clasp to generate multiple style options. Here are some of our favorite ways to wear these necklaces. Have fun discovering your own styles. Make a pair of earrings with the leftover beads.

SUPPLY NOTE
Twister clasps are also called tornado clasps or pearl shorteners.

1 **necklaces •** Cut a piece of beading wire (Basics, p. 12). (My necklaces are 1 yd./.9m.) String five to nine 6mm beads as desired. String a flat spacer.

2 **a** String five to nine 6mm beads as desired. String a round spacer.

b String beads and spacers as in steps 1 and 2a until the strand is within 1 in. (2.5cm) of the finished length.

3 On one end, string a crimp bead. String the other end through the crimp bead plus one more bead. Check the fit. Add or remove beads, if necessary. Tighten the wire and crimp the crimp bead (Basics). Trim the excess wire. Use chainnose pliers to close a crimp cover over the crimp bead.

4 Make a second necklace. To wear the necklaces as a short rope necklace: String both necklaces on a twister clasp, twist the necklaces together, and string the other side of both necklaces on the clasp.

1 earrings • On a head pin, string a 3mm spacer and a 6mm bead. Make a plain loop (Basics, p. 12).

2 Cut a 2-in. (5cm) piece of wire. Make a wrapped loop (Basics). String two 6mms and a spacer. Make a wrapped loop.

3 Open the loop of the small bead unit and attach it to a wrapped loop of the large bead unit. Close the loop.

4 Open the loop of an earring wire (Basics). Attach the dangle and close the loop. Make a second earring to match the first. ❖

Supply List

necklaces
- **4** 16-in. (41cm) strands 6mm beads, in four colors
- **4** 8-in. (20cm) strands 6mm Czech glass beads, in four colors

- **20–40** 6–8mm flat spacers
- **20–40** 3mm round spacers
- flexible beading wire, .014 or .015
- **2** crimp beads
- **2** crimp covers
- twister clasp

(Fire Mountain Gems, 800-355-2137, firemountaingems.com)
- chainnose pliers
- diagonal wire cutters
- crimping pliers (optional)

earrings
- **6** 6mm beads, in three colors

- **4** 3mm round spacers
- 4 in. (10cm) 24-gauge half-hard wire
- **2** 1½-in. (3.8cm) head pins
- pair of earring wires
- chainnose and roundnose pliers
- diagonal wire cutters

Quick mix and match

by Eva Kapitany

Cluster similarly shaped gems for a brilliant necklace

Sparkling gemstone and cubic zirconia beads make a dramatic impact when clustered at the front of a necklace. Use shapes that are similar, such as briolettes, pears, and drops, to pull the look together.

1 **necklace •** Cut a 3-in. (7.6cm) piece of wire. String a top-drilled bead and make a set of wraps (Basics, p. 12). Make the first half of a wrapped loop (Basics) perpendicular to the wraps. Repeat with the remaining top-drilled beads.

2 On a head pin, string a rectangular bead and a crystal. Make the first half of a wrapped loop.

3 Decide how long you want your necklace to be, and cut a piece of chain to that length. (The purple necklace is 16½ in./41.9cm; the green-and-orange necklace is 17½ in./44.5cm.) Attach the largest bead unit to the center link and complete the wraps. Set aside one top-drilled bead unit for step 5. On each side, every ¼–½ in. (6–13mm), attach a bead unit to the chain and complete the wraps.

4 Check the fit, and trim chain from each end if necessary. On one end, open a jump ring (Basics) and attach a lobster claw clasp. Close the jump ring.

5 On the other end, use a jump ring to attach a soldered jump ring. Attach the remaining bead unit to the soldered jump ring and complete the wraps.

SUPPLY NOTE

You can buy cubic zirconia beads from Fusion Beads, 888-781-3559, fusionbeads.com.

EDITOR'S TIP

To keep your necklace well balanced, buy your beads first, then choose a chain that is proportional. If you select heavy beads and chain, use 22-gauge wire and head pins. For a more delicate necklace, use 24 gauge.

Supply List

necklace
- **5** top-drilled beads (briolettes, pears, or drops) in assorted sizes
- **6 x 8mm** rectangular bead
- **4mm** bicone crystal
- **15 in. (38cm)** 22- or 24-gauge half-hard wire
- **16–20 in. (41–51cm)** chain, 2–7mm links
- **2-in. (5cm)** head pin
- **2 4–6mm** jump rings
- lobster claw clasp and soldered jump ring
- chainnose and roundnose pliers
- diagonal wire cutters

earrings
- **2 6–15mm** top-drilled beads
- **6 in. (15cm)** 22- or 24-gauge half-hard wire
- pair of earring threads, with open loops
- chainnose and roundnose pliers
- diagonal wire cutters

1 earrings • Cut a 3-in. (7.6cm) piece of wire. String a top-drilled bead and make a set of wraps (Basics, p. 12). Make a wrapped loop (Basics) perpendicular to the wraps.

2 Open the loop of an earring thread (Basics). Attach the bead unit and close the loop. Make a second earring to match the first. ✤

FALL

for a free-form necklace

by Carol McKinney

Create a multitextured necklace with beads and nuggets

For a fun, free-spirited design, string beads randomly. Or, make the pattern more orderly by planning your bead placement prior to stringing. Either way, the bold, chunky components will brighten winter's subdued hues and complement the season's detailed clothing.

1 Cut a piece of beading wire (Basics, p. 12) for the shortest strand of your necklace. (The shortest strands of my necklaces are 16 in./41cm.) Cut three more pieces, each approximately 2 in. (5cm) longer than the previous piece.

On a head pin or eye pin, string a focal bead. Make a wrapped loop (Basics).

2 On the shortest wire, 3½ in. (8.9cm) from one end, string a round crimp bead, a gemstone bead, and a round crimp bead. Flatten the crimp beads (Basics).

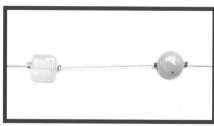

3 Approximately 1–2 in. (2.5–5cm) from the previous bead, string a round crimp bead, a gemstone, and a round crimp bead. Flatten the crimp beads. Repeat three to five times.

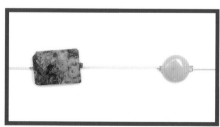

4 On the second wire, 4½ in. (11.4cm) from one end, repeat the pattern in step 3, spacing the beads 1½ –2 in. (3.8–5cm) apart.

154

5 On the third wire, 4 in. (10cm) from one end, repeat the pattern in step 3. Space the beads 2–2½ in. (5–6.4cm) apart.

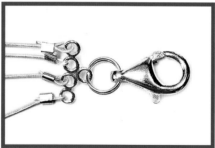

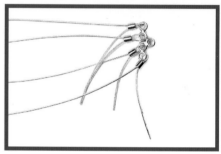

6 On the fourth wire, center a round crimp bead, the focal-bead unit, and a round crimp bead. Flatten the crimp beads. On each end, beginning ¾ in. (1.9cm) from the focal bead, repeat the pattern in step 3. Space the beads 2–2½ in. (5–6.4cm) apart.

7 On each end, string a crimp tube and the corresponding loop of a connector bar. Check the fit, and trim the wires if necessary. Go back through the crimp tube and tighten the wire. Make a folded crimp (Basics), and trim the excess wire.

8 On each end, attach a split ring to the connector bar. On one end, attach a lobster claw clasp to the split ring.

9 String two beads on a head pin or eye pin. Make a wrapped loop. Attach the finished dangle to the split ring. ❖

Supply List

- 30–35mm gemstone focal bead
- **22–30** 10–25mm gemstone beads
- flexible beading wire, .018 or .019
- **2** four-to-one connector bars (Artbeads.com, 866-715-2323)
- **2** 2-in. (5cm) head pins or eye pins
- **2** 6mm split rings
- **42–58** round crimp beads
- **8** crimp tubes
- lobster claw clasp
- chainnose and roundnose pliers
- crimping pliers
- diagonal wire cutters
- split-ring pliers (optional)

Silken knots
tie up Asian style

Capturing the spirit of the East is simple with this necklace-and-earring set

by Irina Miech

A delicately engraved donut and knotted silk ribbons form the basis of a subtle, exotic jewelry set. Try different color choices to change the mood.

3 Determine the finished length of your necklace. (Mine is 17 in./43cm.)

Cut a 4-in. (10cm) piece of 22-gauge wire. Make the first half of a wrapped loop (Basics). String one set of ribbons through the loop, positioning the loop within 2 in. (5cm) of the desired finished length. Repeat on the other side.

1 **necklace •** Fold three silk ribbons in half and string the ends through a donut pendant. Pull the ribbons through the resulting loop.

2 On each side of the pendant, string a large-hole bead on each ribbon. Tie an overhand knot (Basics, p. 12) with all three ribbons. Repeat the pattern twice.

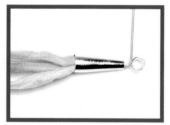

4 On each side, tightly wrap the wire tail around the ribbons. Trim the ribbons ¼ in. (6mm) from the wraps and apply Dritz Fray Check to the ends.

5 On each end, string a cone over the wire stem and make the first half of a wrapped loop.

6 On a head pin, string a 5mm bead. Make the first half of a wrapped loop.
Attach a 2-in. (5cm) chain and complete the wraps.

7 On one end, string the chain extender and complete the wraps. Repeat on the other end, substituting an S-hook clasp for the chain extender.

EDITOR'S TIP
Consider using large-hole silver spacers instead of faceted beads for greater visual contrast.

Supply List

necklace
- 40mm engraved donut pendant (Eclectica, 262-641-0910)
- **18** 8–10mm large-hole, faceted round beads (Eclectica)
- 5mm round bead
- 8 in. (20cm) 22-gauge half-hard wire
- **3** 18–22-in. (46–56cm) silk ribbons (Eclectica)
- 2 in. (5cm) chain, 4–5mm links
- 1½-in. (3.8cm) head pin
- **2** 12mm cones
- S-hook clasp

- chainnose and roundnose pliers
- diagonal wire cutters
- Dritz Fray Check

earrings
- **2** 10mm large-hole, faceted round beads (Eclectica, 262-641-0910)
- 6 in. (15cm) 24-gauge half-hard wire
- 7 in. (18cm) silk ribbon (Eclectica)
- **2** 12mm cones
- pair of earring wires
- chainnose and roundnose pliers
- diagonal wire cutters
- Dritz Fray Check

1 **earrings** • Cut a 3½-in. (8.9cm) piece of silk ribbon. Center a bead on the ribbon.

2 Cut a 3-in. (7.6cm) piece of 22-gauge wire. Make the first half of a wrapped loop (Basics, p. 12). String the ribbon ends through the loop. Tightly wrap the wire tail around the ribbons. Trim the ends ⅛ in. (3mm) from the wraps and apply Dritz Fray Check to the ends.

3 String a cone on the wire. Make a wrapped loop.

4 Open the loop of an earring wire (Basics). Attach the dangle and close the loop. Make a second earring to match the first. ❖

Curved in **stone**

Twist nuggets, faceted
rondelles, and curved tube
beads in a spectacular
two-strand necklace

by Debbi Simon

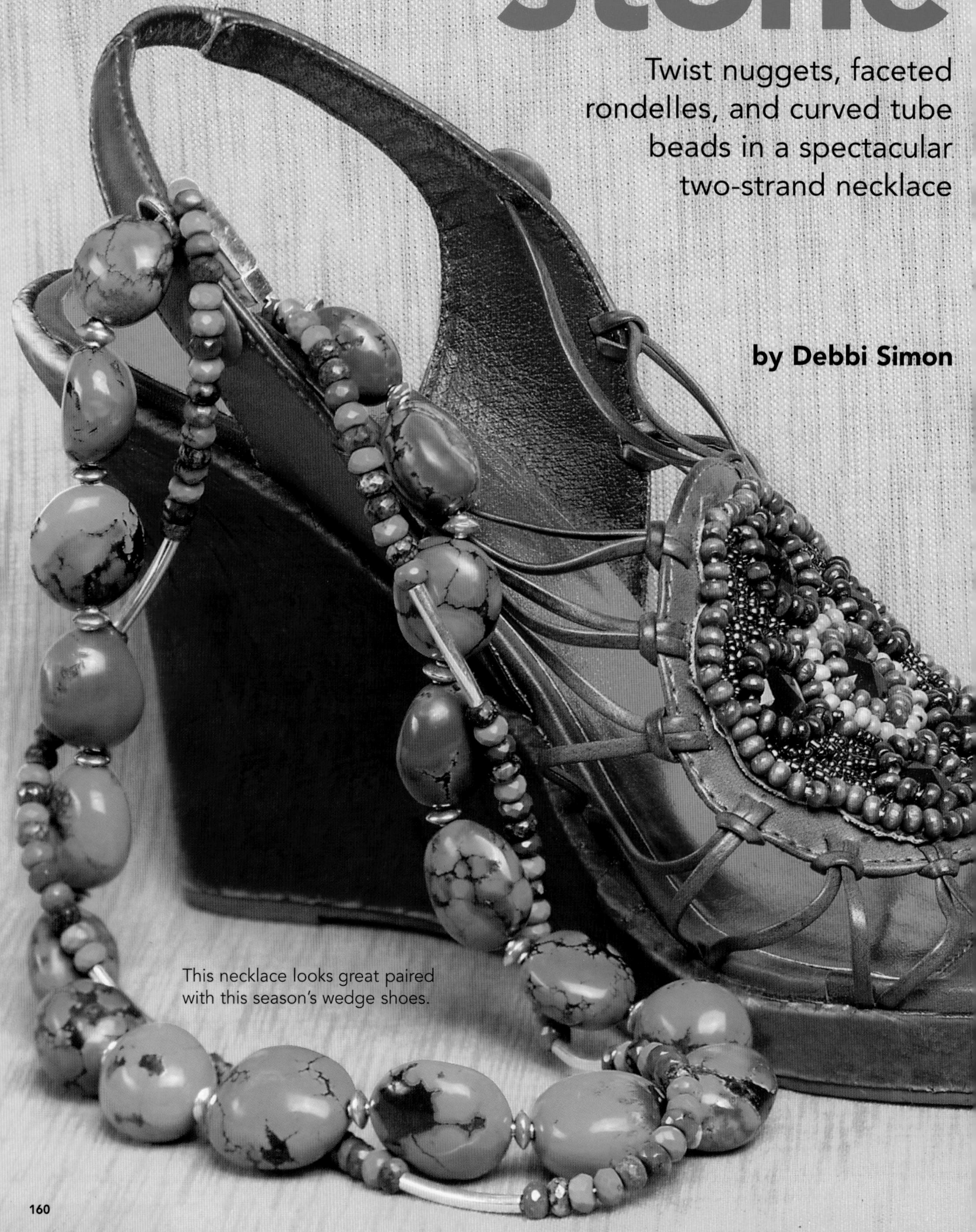

This necklace looks great paired
with this season's wedge shoes.

String turquoise nuggets with a matching strand of faceted rondelles and curved tube beads. Or, try a combination of deep-colored amber nuggets with rondelles in a more subtle shade. Twist the strands together before clasping the necklace for an impressive piece that is sure to be a classic.

1 Cut a piece of beading wire (Basics, p. 12). (The amber necklace is 17½ in./44.5cm; the turquoise, 19 in./48cm.) Cut another piece 2 in. (5cm) longer. Center a nugget on the shorter wire.

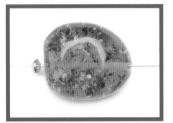

2 On each end, string a saucer and a nugget, repeating until the strand is within 1 in. (2.5cm) of the desired length. End with a nugget.

3 On each end, string a bead cap, a round spacer, a crimp bead, a spacer, and one loop of half of a clasp. Go back through the beads just strung and tighten the wire.

EDITOR'S TIP
Showcase a distinctive clasp by wearing it slightly off center, toward the front of your necklace.

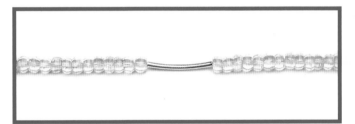

4 On the longer wire, string 2½ in. (6.4cm) of rondelles, a curved tube bead, and 2½ in. (6.4cm) of rondelles. Center the beads on the wire.

5 On each end, string a tube and 2½ in. (6.4cm) of rondelles, repeating until the strand is 1½ in. (3.8cm) longer than the first strand. End with rondelles.

6 On each end, string a spacer, a crimp bead, a spacer, and the remaining loop of half of the clasp. Go back through the last few beads strung and tighten the wires. Check the fit, and add or remove beads from each end if necessary. Crimp the crimp beads (Basics) and trim the excess wire. ❖

Supply List

- 16-in. (41cm) strand 20mm gemstone nuggets
- 4–6 22–26mm curved tube beads (Fire Mountain Gems, 800-355-2137, firemoutaingems.com)
- 16-in. (41cm) strand 6mm faceted rondelles
- 14–20 5–6mm saucer spacers
- 8 3mm round spacers

- 2 10mm bead caps
- flexible beading wire, .018 or .019
- 4 crimp beads
- two-strand box clasp (square clasp from Singaraja Imports, singarajaimports.com; round clasp from Jess Imports, jessimports.com)
- chainnose or crimping pliers
- diagonal wire cutters

Create a fresh look with leafy beads

Go from wish list to gift in a flash with this easy bracelet

by Jeanne Gassert

This one-of-a-kind gift is the perfect solution for a last-minute invitation. Use marquise-cut stones to create a look that can be made in colors for every season.

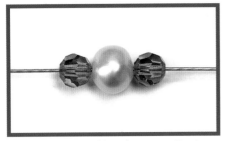

1 Cut a piece of beading wire (Basics, p. 12). On the wire, center a crystal, a pearl, and a crystal.

2 String four marquise-cut gemstones, alternating their positions as shown. String the pearl/crystal pattern and gemstone pattern three or more times, ending with a crystal, until the bracelet is within 1 in. (2.5cm) of the desired length.

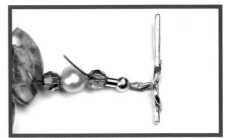

3 On each end, string a crimp bead, a spacer, and half of a clasp. Check the fit, and add or remove beads from each end if necessary. Go back through the beads just strung and tighten the wire. Crimp the crimp beads (Basics) and trim the excess wire. ❖

SupplyList

- 12-in. (30cm) strand 8 x 15mm marquise-cut gemstones, top drilled)
- 10–12 4mm round crystals
- 5–6 6mm potato-shaped pearls
- 2 3mm round spacers
- flexible beading wire, .014 or .015
- 2 crimp beads
- toggle clasp
- chainnose or crimping pliers
- diagonal wire cutters

EDITOR'S TIP
Consider mixing smooth and faceted gemstones or alternating colors to create an unexpected visual dynamic.

Shortcuts

Readers' tips to make your beading life easier

1 festive packaging
Use plastic Easter eggs or jelly beans as small gift boxes. They're also a great way to transport your jewelry to bead shows or package it for buyers.
– *Marcy Whiteside, Delta Junction, Ala.*

2 quick clips
I use binder clips to hold beads on a wire while working on a project. The clips keep the beads from sliding off and are easy to remove and clamp back on.
– *Cheryl Wilson, Blaine, Minn.*

3 notes to self
I always have sticky notes and a pen on hand when I read *BeadStyle*. I write my ideas for gifts or project inspirations and tab the pages to refer back to later.
– *Margret Avedisian, Selma, Calif.*

4 secure crimps
For secure finishing on my necklaces and bracelets, I flatten the crimp bead slightly before stringing it on the wire. This makes it easier to make sure I have one strand of wire on each side of the crimp bead's crease when I crimp it completely.
– *Rose Ann Gussy, via e-mail*

5 instant inspiration
I keep a pretty container of two matching beads from each new strand in my collection. It's a great source for quick earring gifts or color-accent ideas for a new project.
– *Jackie Lapham, Isabella, Calif.*

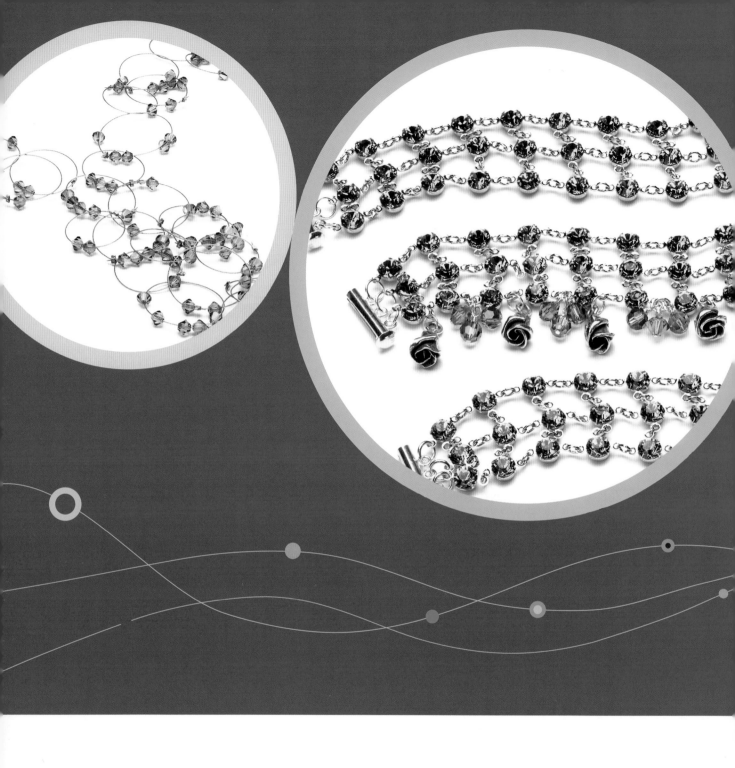

Crystals

Matching bracelets
lead a double life

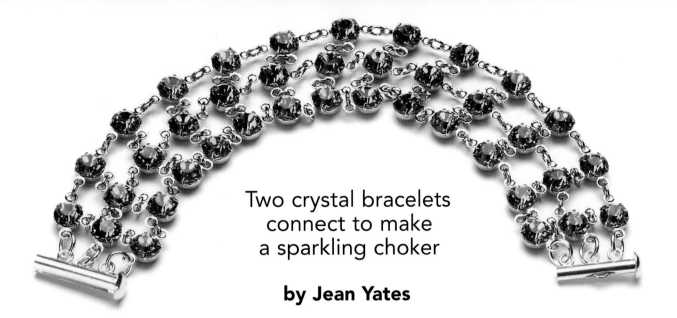

Two crystal bracelets connect to make a sparkling choker

by Jean Yates

Premade crystal webbing puts instant glamour at your fingertips. Each of these easy bracelets — one with dangles, one without — is beautiful in its own right. But link them, and you have a glittering multistrand choker. Add quick dangle earrings to complete the ensemble.

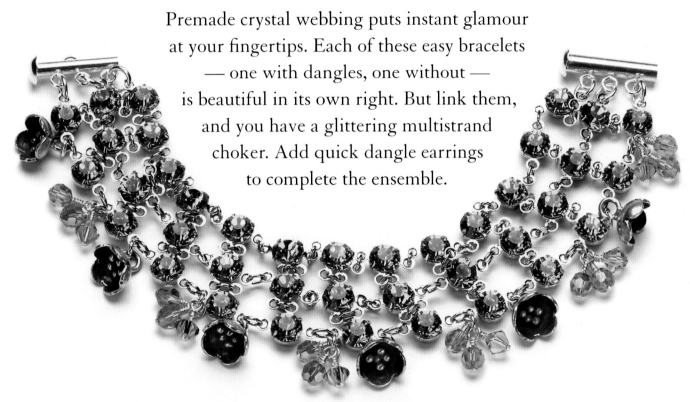

1 **bracelets/necklace** • Decide how long you want your bracelets to be. Make sure the two bracelets are long enough to make a necklace when you connect them. (My bracelets are 7¾ in./19.7cm.) For each bracelet: Cut a 6½–8-in. (16.5–20cm) piece of webbing by removing the jump rings between the columns. Open six 6mm jump rings (Basics, p. 12). Attach the end loops of each piece of webbing and the corresponding loops of half of a clasp. Close the jump rings.

2 String a round crystal on a head pin. Make a wrapped loop (Basics). Repeat with a bicone crystal. Make 12 to 16 round-crystal units and six to eight bicone units.

Supply List

bracelets/necklace
- **6–8** 10–15mm charms
- **12–16** 5–6mm round crystals
- **6–8** 5–6mm bicone crystals
- **14–17** in. (36–43cm) crystal webbing
- **18–24** 1½-in. (3.8cm) head pins
- **12** 6mm jump rings
- **12–16** 4mm jump rings
- **2** three-strand slide clasps
- chainnose and roundnose pliers
- diagonal wire cutters

earrings
- **2** 10–15mm charms
- **4** 5–6mm round crystals
- **2** 5–6mm bicone crystals
- **2** links of crystal webbing
- **2¼** in. (5.7cm) cable chain, 4mm links
- **6** 1½-in. (3.8cm) head pins
- **4** 4mm jump rings
- pair of earring wires
- chainnose and roundnose pliers
- diagonal wire cutters

3 On one bracelet, open a 4mm jump ring. Attach a charm to the loop to the right of the first link. Close the jump ring. Repeat along the bottom, skipping every other rhinestone.

4 Use a 4mm jump ring to attach two round-crystal units and a bicone unit to the loop to the left of the third rhinestone. Repeat along the bottom, skipping every other link.

SUPPLY NOTES
All supplies are available at Fusion Beads, 888-781-3559, fusionbeads.com. Three-row Swarovski-crystal webbing is sold by the link (column). Each link consists of three vertically connected rhinestones. When you purchase multiple links, they come connected with jump rings. In the brown necklace, I used topaz webbing, topaz bicones, and round crystals in light Colorado topaz and light smoked topaz. In the blue necklace, I used light sapphire webbing and bicones and peridot round crystals.

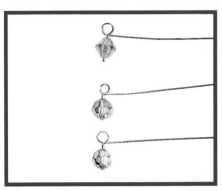

1 earrings • From a column of three rhinestones, remove the center rhinestone unit.

2 Cut a 1-in. (2.5cm) piece of chain. Open a 4mm jump ring (Basics, p. 12). Attach a charm to the chain. Close the jump ring.

3 String a bicone crystal on a head pin. Make the first half of a wrapped loop (Basics). Repeat with two round crystals.

4 Attach the crystal units to the chain as shown. Complete the wraps. Use a jump ring to attach the chain to a loop of the rhinestone unit.

5 Open the loop of an earring wire (Basics). Attach the dangle and close the loop. Make a second earring to match the first. ❖

Twist toge
a crystal illusion

Knots create a zigzag pattern

by Teresa Kodatt

Well-placed knots create new angles for an airy illusion necklace. Twist together three strands for a twinkling tangle of color and light.

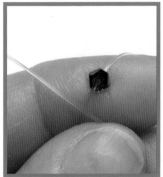

1 Cut a 5-ft. (1.5m) piece of monofilament. Center a crystal and position it on your index finger. Wrap the monofilament around your index finger and to the left of the crystal to form a loop around your finger and over the monofilament below the crystal.

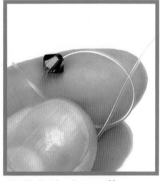

2 Slide the loop off your finger and string the monofilament through the loop from front to back.

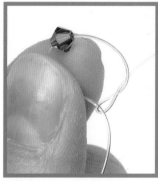

3 Making sure the loop stays behind the crystal, hold the crystal while pulling the ends of the monofilament to tighten the knot.

4 Pull the ends to tighten the knot further.

5 With the crystal angled up, knot another crystal (as in steps 1–4) ½ in. (1.3cm) from the first.

6 Continue knotting crystals for approximately 5 in. (13cm). Repeat on the other end until the crystal section is approximately 10 in. (25cm) long.

ther necklace

171

EDITOR'S TIP
Practice tying knots on a scrap piece of monofilament before starting the necklace.

7 Make two more strands, alternating crystals and groups of three 11º seed beads.

SupplyList

- **2** 7mm large-hole beads
- **90–110** 4mm crystals
- **4g** 11º seed beads
- **5** yd. (4.6m) monofilament, 17 lb. weight
- **6–10** in. (15–25cm) cable chain, 4mm links

- **4** 4–5mm jump rings
- **2** crimp ends with loops, 0.8mm inside diameter
- lobster claw clasp and soldered jump ring
- chainnose and roundnose pliers
- diagonal wire cutters

8 On each end, string the three strands through a crimp end. Flatten the crimp portion (Basics, p. 12).

9 On each end, trim the excess monofilament. Slide a large-hole bead over the crimp end. Squeeze the loop slightly to accommodate the bead, if necessary.

10 Cut two 3–5-in. (7.6–13cm) pieces of chain. (My necklace is 16 in./41cm.) On each end, open a jump ring (Basics) and attach a chain and a crimp end's loop. Close the jump ring.

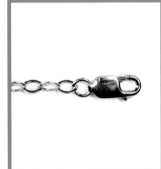

11 On one end, use a jump ring to attach the chain to a lobster claw clasp. Repeat on the other end, substituting a soldered jump ring for the clasp. ❖

Crystals add
spark
to silk

Shimmering dangles contrast with this necklace's soft macramé cord

by Monica Lueder

It takes opposing elements to pull this necklace together. Silk cord adds a soft twist of matte color that won't overpower the subtle shimmer of faceted beads. Likewise, the organic variation in the knots balances the symmetry of the cut crystals. This attraction of opposites will guarantee a dynamic look for any occasion.

1 String a faceted bead on a 2-in. (5cm) head pin and make a wrapped loop (Basics, p. 12). Make 18 to 32 bead units.

2 To knot the silk cords: Bring the left cord over and around the right cord and then over itself. Tighten the knot. Bring the right cord over and around the left and then over itself. Tighten the knot. Continue knotting with alternating cords until the strand is within 1 in. (2.5cm) of the desired length. (My necklaces are 14½ in./36.8cm.)

3 Open a jump ring (Basics) and attach a bead unit to a knotted loop at the center of the necklace. Close the jump ring.

4 On each side, attach bead units to the cord at ½-in. (1.3cm) intervals. Check the fit, allowing 1 in. (2.5cm) for finishing on each end. Add or untie knots, if necessary.

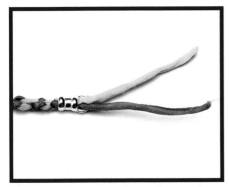

5 On each side, tie the ends together in an overhand knot (Basics). Apply glue to the knot, and string a crimp end so the knot is centered within it.

6 On each end, trim the cords near the crimp end. Flatten the center section of the crimp end with chainnose pliers.

7 Open a jump ring and attach an S-hook clasp and one of the crimp ends. Close the jump ring. Repeat on the other end, substituting a soldered jump ring for the clasp. ❖

Supply**List**

- **18–32** faceted rectangular beads
- **2** 18–22-in. (46–56cm) silk cords, in two colors
- **18–32** 2-in. (5cm) head pins
- **20–34** 6mm inside diameter (ID) jump rings
- **2** 5mm crimp ends
- S-hook clasp and 6mm ID soldered jump ring
- chainnose and roundnose pliers
- diagonal wire cutters
- E6000 adhesive

DESIGN GUIDELINES
- To add more color, braid three strands of cord.
- If you use soldered jump rings, string the bead units as you make the knots. When making the dangles, make the first half of a wrapped loop. Attach the jump ring and then complete the wraps.

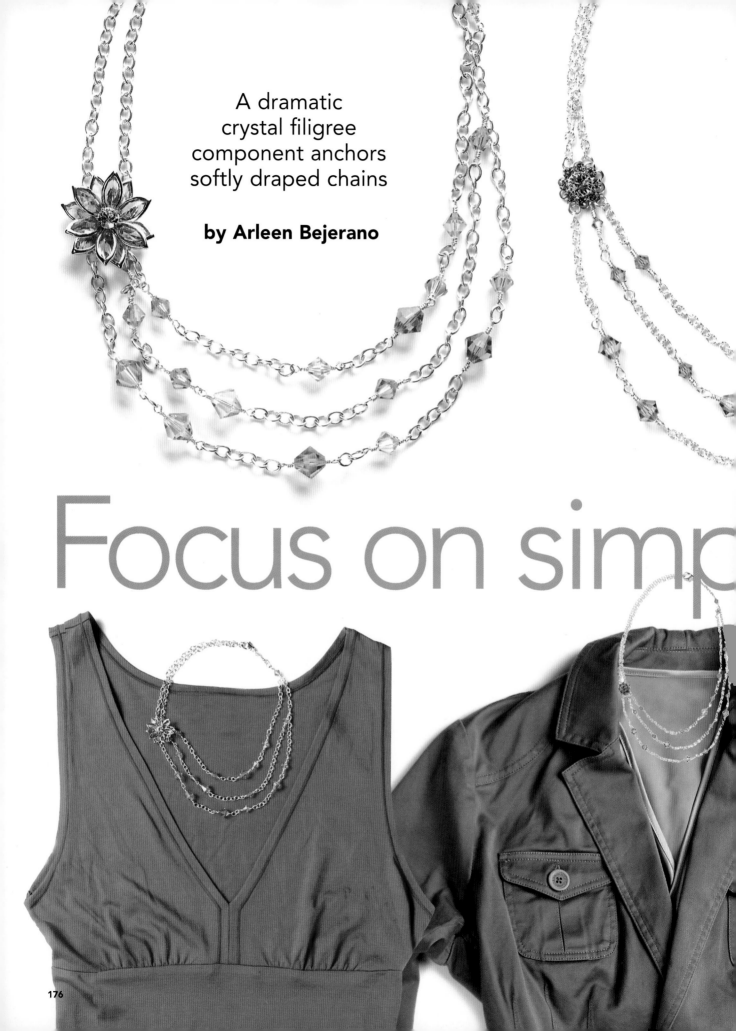

A dramatic
crystal filigree
component anchors
softly draped chains

by Arleen Bejerano

Focus on simp

When you have a beautiful focal point, it's smart to keep things simple, but never ordinary. This contemporary necklace has an off-center centerpiece, delicate chains, and bicones of coordinating colors.

le elegance

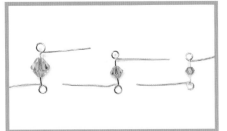

1 **necklace** • Cut a 2½-in. (6.4cm) piece of wire. Make the first half of a wrapped loop (Basics, p. 12) on one end. String a large bicone crystal. Make the first half of a wrapped loop. Make six large-bicone units, 11 medium-bicone units, and three small-bicone units.

2 Cut a 10–14-in. (25–36cm) piece of chain, depending on the desired length of your necklace. (My necklaces are 15 in./38cm and use a 10-in./25cm chain.) Open two 2mm jump rings (Basics) and attach each end of the chain and a loop of the filigree component as shown. Close the jump rings.

3 String a 4mm jump ring through the two center links of the chain.

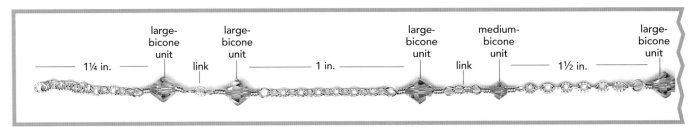

large-bicone unit — 1¼ in. — large-bicone unit — link — 1 in. — large-bicone unit — link — medium-bicone unit — 1½ in. — large-bicone unit

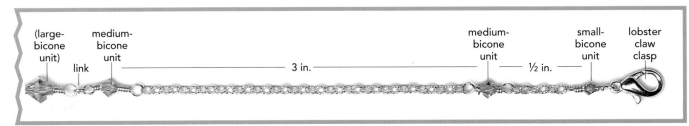

(large-bicone unit) — link — medium-bicone unit — 3 in. — medium-bicone unit — ½ in. — small-bicone unit — lobster claw clasp

4 To make the longest strand: Cut chains to the lengths shown. Attach components as shown. Attach a lobster claw clasp to the end loop of the small-bicone unit. Complete the wraps.

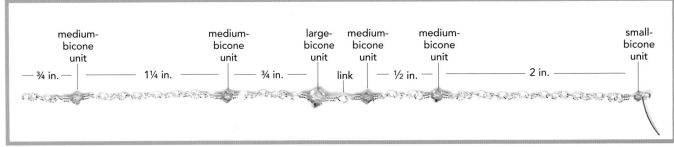

medium-bicone unit — ¾ in. — 1¼ in. — medium-bicone unit — ¾ in. — large-bicone unit — link — medium-bicone unit — ½ in. — medium-bicone unit — 2 in. — small-bicone unit

5 To make the shortest strand: Cut chains to the lengths shown. Attach components as shown. Complete the wraps, leaving the end loop of the small-bicone unit open.

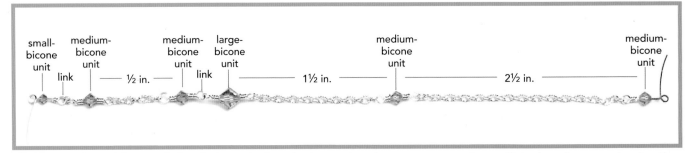

small-bicone unit — link — medium-bicone unit — ½ in. — medium-bicone unit — link — large-bicone unit — 1½ in. — medium-bicone unit — 2½ in. — medium-bicone unit

6 To make the middle strand: Cut chains to the lengths shown. Attach components as shown. Complete the wraps, leaving the end loops open.

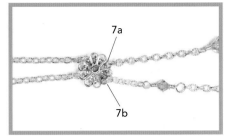

7a Use a 2mm jump ring to attach the longest strand and a loop of the filigree component.

b Use a 2mm jump ring to attach the end link of the shortest strand and a loop of the filigree component.

8 Attach the small-bicone unit of the middle strand to the filigree-component loop used in step 7b. Complete the wraps.

9 Attach the small-bicone unit of the shortest strand to the loop of the medium-bicone unit of the longest strand nearest the clasp. Complete the wraps.

10 Attach the medium-bicone unit of the middle strand to the longest strand approximately 2½ in. (6.4cm) from the clasp. Complete the wraps.

EDITOR'S TIP

Using proportional bicone crystals balances this necklace. For the larger pink filigree component, the bicones are 10mm, 8mm, and 4mm. For the green component, the bicones are 8mm, 4mm, and 3mm.

1 earrings • String a large bicone crystal on a head pin. Make the first half of a wrapped loop (Basics, p. 12). Cut a 1-in. (2.5cm) piece of chain.

2 Open a 2mm jump ring (Basics). Attach the chain and a filigree component. Close the jump ring. Attach the bicone unit to the remaining end of the chain. Complete the wraps.

3 Use a jump ring to attach the dangle and the loop of an earring post. Make a second earring to match the first. ❖

SupplyList

necklace
• crystal filigree component (25mm component from Chic Beads, chicbeads.com; 11mm component from Jewelry Supply Inc., jewelrysupply.com)
• **6** 8–10mm bicone crystals
• **11** 4–8mm bicone crystals
• **3** 3–4mm bicone crystals
• 45–50 in. (1.1–1.3m) 24-gauge half-hard wire
• 1 yd. (.9m) cable chain, 3–4mm links
• **4** 2mm jump rings
• lobster claw clasp and 4mm jump ring
• chainnose and roundnose pliers
• diagonal wire cutters

earrings
• 2 crystal filigree components (Jewelry Supply Inc., jewelrysupply.com)
• 2 8mm bicone crystals
• 2 in. (5cm) cable chain, 3–4mm links
• 2 2-in. (5cm) head pins
• **4** 2mm jump rings
• pair of earring posts with ear nuts
• chainnose and roundnose pliers
• diagonal wire cutters

Marcasite & crystals make an opulent bracelet

Intricate marcasite beads add texture • by Gloria Farver

Balancing marcasite with crystals enhances sparkle and makes this elegant bracelet affordable. A series of well-formed wrapped loops ties the look together.

Supply**List**

- marcasite beads:
  - 8 x 18mm teardrop shaped
  - **2** or **4** 6 x 8mm rounds (**2** for a 7-in./18cm bracelet, **4** for an 8½-in./21.6cm bracelet)
  - 2 4 x 8mm rectangles
  - 4 4 x 6mm rounds
- **25–30** 4mm bicone crystals
- **2–4** 3mm flat silver spacers
- 3½ ft. (1.1m) 22- or 24-gauge half-hard wire
- **4–6** 2½-in. (6.4cm) head pins
- marcasite toggle clasp
- chainnose and roundnose pliers
- diagonal wire cutters

EDITOR'S TIP

The finished bracelet measures 8½ in. (21.6cm). For a 7-in. (18cm) bracelet, begin and end with 6 x 8mm components.

1 To make the dangles, string a bicone crystal, a rectangular marcasite bead, and a bicone on a head pin. Make the first half of a wrapped loop (Basics, p. 12). Make a total of two marcasite dangles.

On a head pin, string a bicone, a flat spacer, and a bicone. Make the first half of a wrapped loop. Make a total of four crystal dangles.

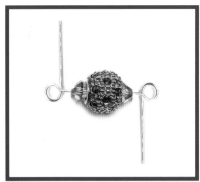

2 Cut eight 3½-in. (8.9cm) pieces of wire. Make the first half of a wrapped loop on one end of each. String a bicone, a 4 x 6mm bead, and a bicone on four of the wires. String a bicone, a 6 x 8mm bead, and a bicone on the remaining wires. Make the first half of a wrapped loop on the end of each.

Cut a 4½-in. (11.4cm) piece of wire. Make the first half of a wrapped loop. String a bicone, an 8 x 18mm bead, and a bicone. Make the first half of a wrapped loop.

3 Attach half of a toggle clasp to a loop of one of the 4 x 6mm-bead units. Complete the wraps.

4 Attach the loop of a 6 x 8mm unit to the previous unit. Complete the wraps.

Attach a 4 x 6mm unit to the previous unit. Complete the wraps. Attach a 6 x 8mm unit to the previous unit. Complete the wraps.

5 Repeat steps 3 and 4 with the remaining half of the clasp.

Attach each loop of the 8 x 18mm unit to the available loops on each half of the bracelet. Complete the wraps.

6 Attach one marcasite and two crystal dangles between the third and fourth components from each end (between the second and third components if you make a 7-in./18cm bracelet). Complete the wraps. ❖

An intricate choker is perfect
for a formal occasion

by **Kathie Scrimgeour**

For a

special day

To accessorize a picture-perfect bride on her special day, incorporate distinctive materials, including beading chain, specialty tube beads, and crystals. Use small tube beads and clear crystals for a wedding, or try larger tube beads and darker crystals for a dressy necklace that's less formal.

1 Decide how long you want your necklace to be. (My necklaces are 17 in./43cm.) Double that measurement, add 12 in. (30cm), and cut two pieces of beading wire to that length. Cut two pieces of beading chain, each 1 in. (2.5cm) longer than the finished length.

On each wire, string one side of an X-tube bead. Center the bead on the wires.

SupplyList

Tube beads from Fire Mountain Gems, 800-355-2137, firemountaingems.com.
- **15–17** 5–12mm X-tube beads
- **32–36** 9 x 1.5mm two-strand curved tube beads
- **30–34** 4mm bicone crystals
- **40–44** 3mm bicone crystals
- **8** 4mm round beads
- **152–176** 3mm round beads
- flexible beading wire, .010 or .012
- 36–40 in. (.9–1m) beading chain
- **2** crimp beads
- **4** crimp covers
- toggle clasp
- chainnose pliers
- diagonal wire cutters
- crimping pliers (optional)

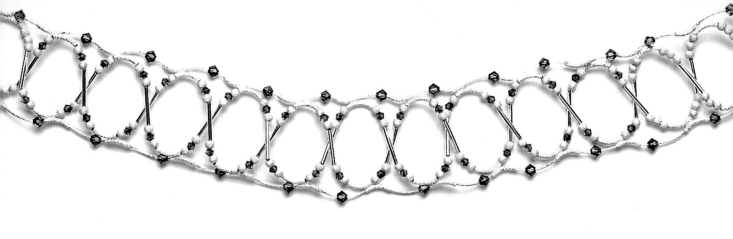

2 On each end of each wire, string: 3mm round bead, 3mm bicone crystal, 3mm round, one side of a curved tube bead, 3mm round, 3mm bicone, 3mm round, one side of an X tube. Repeat until the strands are within 8 in. (20cm) of the finished length.

3 On each end of each wire, string: three 3mm rounds, one side of a curved tube, three 3mm rounds, one side of an X tube. Repeat until the strands are within 3 in. (7.6cm) of the finished length. End with three 3mm rounds.

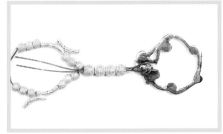

4 On each side, over both wires, string four 4mm round beads, a crimp bead, and half of a clasp. Check the fit, and add or remove beads from each end if necessary. Go back through the beads just strung and tighten the wires, leaving approximately ⅜ in. (1cm) between the crimp bead and the clasp. Crimp the crimp bead (Basics, p. 12) and trim the excess wire.

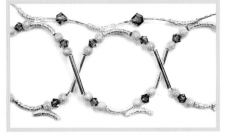

5 Along the top strand, string beading chain through the remaining side of a curved tube, and then string a 4mm bicone crystal. Repeat until you've strung all the curved tubes along the top strand.

EDITOR'S TIP
To make sure that the necklace curves properly, string the two-strand curved tube beads in the same direction.

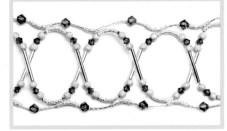

6 Along the bottom strand, string the curved tubes and crystals with the remaining piece of beading chain.

7 On each end, use chainnose pliers to close a crimp cover over the crimp bead and chains. Close an additional crimp cover over the chains and the exposed beading wire. Trim the excess chain. ❖

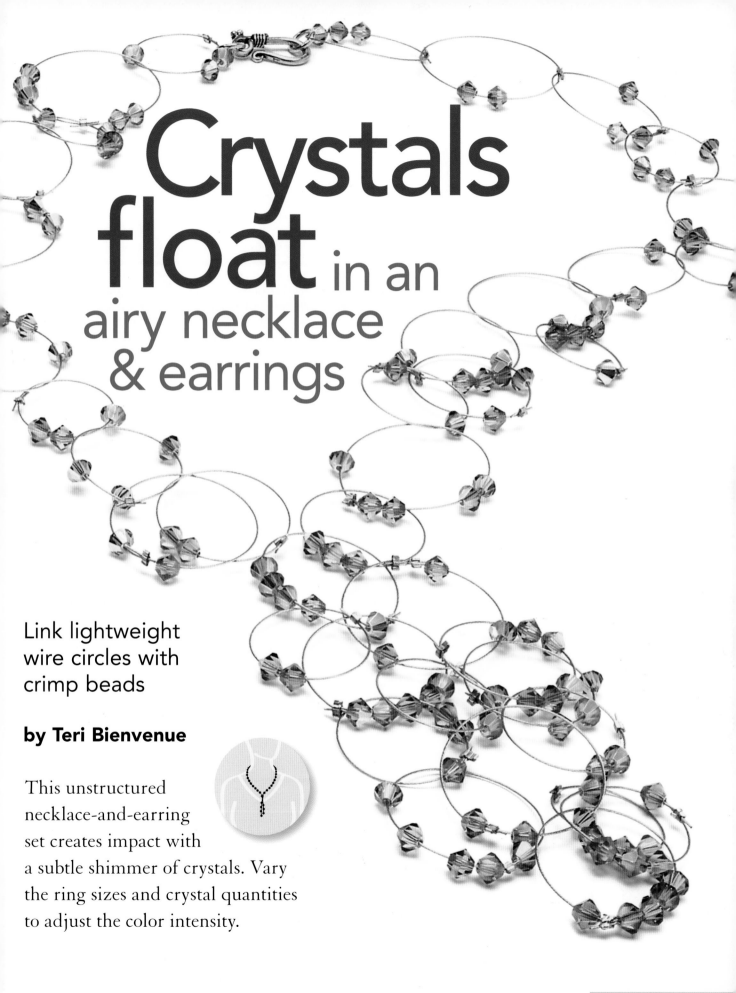

Crystals
float in an
airy necklace
& earrings

**Link lightweight
wire circles with
crimp beads**

by Teri Bienvenue

This unstructured
necklace-and-earring
set creates impact with
a subtle shimmer of crystals. Vary
the ring sizes and crystal quantities
to adjust the color intensity.

1 necklace • Cut a 4-in. (10cm) piece of beading wire. String two crystals. String both ends through a crimp bead, making a loop. Crimp the crimp bead (Basics, p. 12) and trim the ends of the wire close to the crimp.

2 Cut a 4-in. (10cm) piece of beading wire. String three crystals, a crimp bead, and the previous loop. Crimp as in step 1.

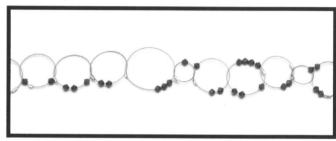

3 Repeat step 2, varying the size of the loops and the number of crystals, until the strand is within 2 in. (5cm) of the desired length. (My necklaces are 17½ in./44.5cm.)

4 On one end, attach a small loop as in step 2, but string a lobster claw or hook clasp before crimping. Repeat on the other end, substituting a soldered jump ring for the clasp.

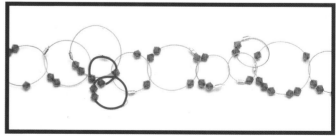

5 Spread out the strand, and attach four or five more loops as desired. Space the groupings evenly along the strand.

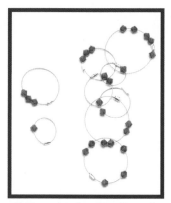

6 To make the dangle, make two single loops and a grouping as desired.

Supply List

necklace
- **100–120** 4mm bicone crystals
- flexible beading wire, .014 or .015
- **36–42** crimp beads
- lobster claw or hook clasp and soldered jump ring
- chainnose or crimping pliers
- diagonal wire cutters

earrings
- 16 4mm bicone crystals
- flexible beading wire, .014 or .015
- 6 crimp beads
- pair of earring wires
- chainnose and roundnose pliers
- diagonal wire cutters
- crimping pliers (optional)

EDITOR'S TIP

Trim the beading wire close to the crimp bead, but allow a little wire to extend so that the crimps are secure.

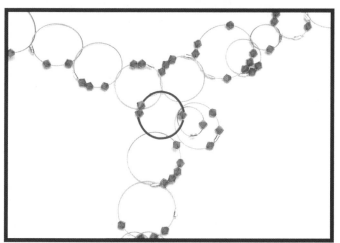

7 Make a single loop and, before crimping, string the center loops of the strand, the dangle, and the two single loops as shown.

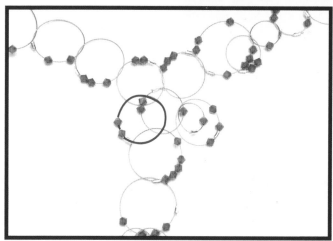

8 Make another single loop and, before crimping, string the dangle and the strand as shown.

Add matching earrings for a lightweight wash of color.

1 **earrings** • Repeat step 1 of the necklace, but string four crystals instead of two. Make a one-crystal loop and a three-crystal loop, linking each to the four-crystal loop.

2 Open the loop of an earring wire (Basics, p. 12). Attach the dangle and close the loop. Make a second earring to match the first. ✤

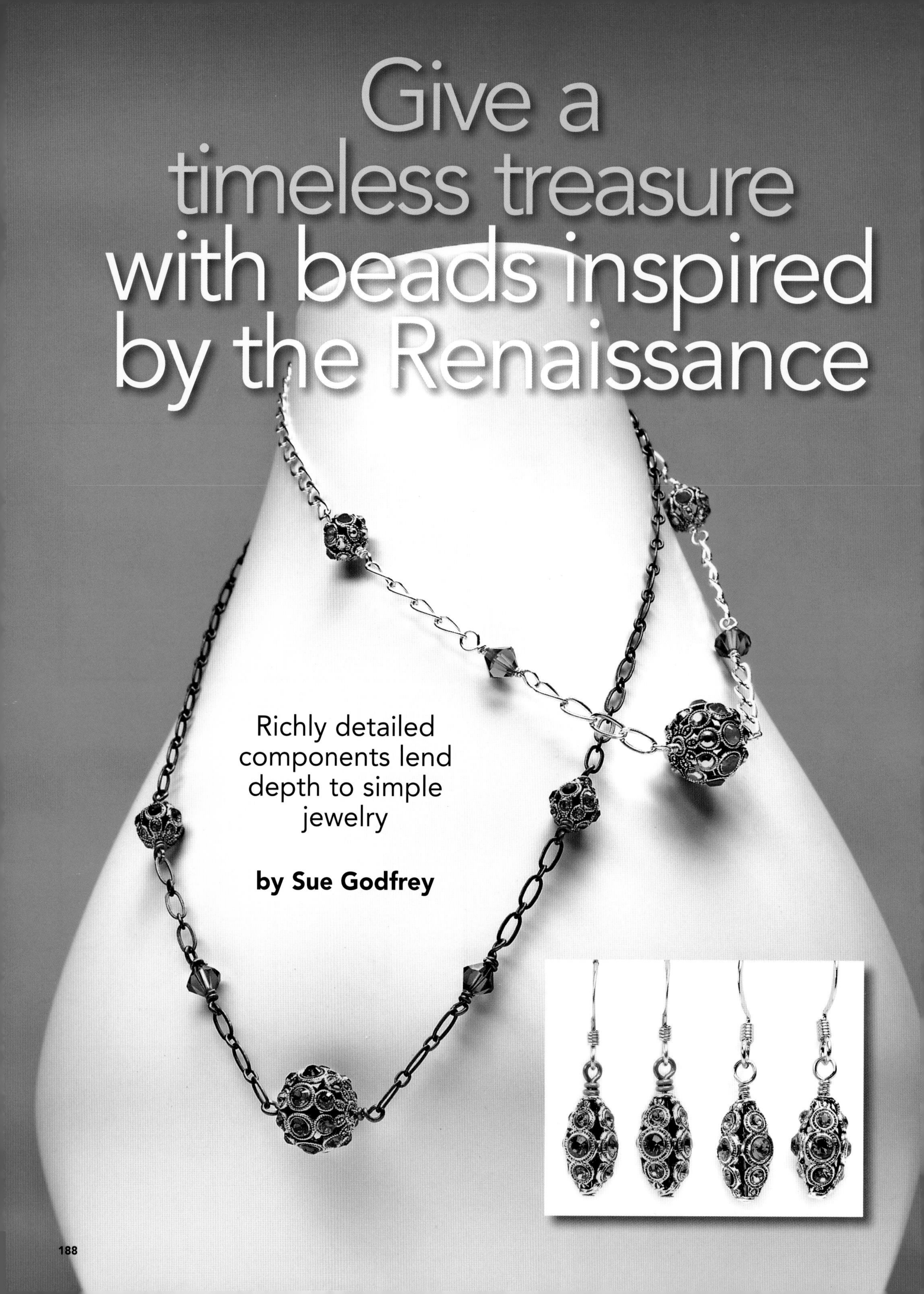

Give a timeless treasure with beads inspired by the Renaissance

Richly detailed components lend depth to simple jewelry

by Sue Godfrey

Crystal-encrusted beads give this necklace-and-earring set a Renaissance look. Consider pairing the beads with brass or oxidized chain to emphasize their antique style. While the jewelry is timeless, the creation of these beautiful pieces will take less than an hour.

1 necklace • Cut a 3-in. (7.6cm) piece of 24-gauge wire. Make the first half of a wrapped loop (Basics, p. 12) on one end. String a 13mm crystal-encrusted bead. Make the first half of a wrapped loop. Repeat with the 8mm crystal-encrusted beads and the bicone crystals.

2 Cut two 1-in. (2.5cm) pieces of chain. Attach a chain to each loop of the 13mm-bead unit. Complete the wraps.

3 Attach a bicone unit to one end of the strand. Cut a 1-in. (2.5cm) piece of chain. Attach the chain to the remaining loop of the bicone unit. Complete the wraps. Repeat on the other side.

4 Attach an 8mm-bead unit to each end. Determine the finished length of your necklace. (Mine is 18 in./46cm.) Subtract the current length of the strand, and cut a piece of chain to that length. Cut the chain in half. Attach a chain to the remaining loop of each 8mm-bead unit. Complete the wraps. Check the fit, and trim chain from each end if necessary.

Supply List

necklace
- 13mm round crystal-encrusted bead (Midwest Beads, midwestbeads.com)
- 2 8mm round crystal-encrusted beads (Midwest Beads, midwestbeads.com)
- 2 6mm bicone crystals
- 15 in. (38cm) 24-gauge half-hard wire
- 15–17 in. (38–43cm) chain, 4mm links
- 2 3–4mm jump rings
- lobster claw clasp and soldered jump ring
- chainnose and roundnose pliers
- diagonal wire cutters

earrings
- 2 13mm oval crystal-encrusted beads (Midwest Beads, midwestbeads.com)
- 2 2-in. (5cm) head pins
- pair of earring wires
- chainnose and roundnose pliers
- diagonal wire cutters

5 Open a jump ring (Basics). Attach a lobster claw clasp and one end of the strand. Close the jump ring. Repeat on the other end, substituting a soldered jump ring for the clasp.

EDITOR'S TIP
To make longer earrings, attach a piece of chain to the bead unit before completing the wraps.

1 earrings • String a crystal-encrusted bead on a head pin. Make a wrapped loop (Basics, p. 12).

2 Open the loop of an earring wire (Basics) and attach the dangle. Close the loop. Make a second earring to match the first. ❖

String a
splash
of crystals

Go glamorous with a high-gleam necklace and earrings

by Irina Miech

Mix a trio of crystal shapes with silver accents to create jewelry that reflects elegance with every facet. Keeping the colors in the same family creates a subtle glow.

1 necklace • On a head pin, string a bicone crystal, a round crystal, and a spacer. Make a wrapped loop (Basics, p. 12). Make a total of 64 crystal units.

2 Cut a piece of beading wire to the desired length of the necklace (Basics). (My necklaces are 16½ in./ 41.9cm.) Center a 16mm pear-shaped crystal on the wire.

3 On each end, string 16 crystal units and a 16mm pear-shaped crystal.

4 On each end, string 16 crystal units and an 11mm pear-shaped crystal.

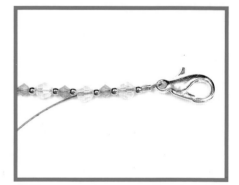

5 On each end, string a spacer, a round crystal, a spacer, and a bicone. Repeat until the strand is within ½ in. (1.3cm) of the finished length. End with a spacer.

6 On a head pin, string a bicone, a round crystal, and a spacer. Make the first half of a wrapped loop. Cut a 2-in. (5cm) piece of chain. Attach the crystal unit and complete the wraps.

7 On one end, string a crimp bead and a lobster claw clasp. Repeat on the other end, substituting the chain for the clasp.

Check the fit, and add or remove beads from each end if necessary. Go back through the beads just strung and tighten the wire. Crimp the crimp beads (Basics) and trim the excess wire.

1 earrings • On a head pin, string a bicone crystal and a round spacer. Make a wrapped loop (Basics, p. 12). Make a total of nine to 12 crystal units.

2 Cut a 4-in. (10cm) piece of wire. String an 11mm pear-shaped crystal and make a set of wraps above it (Basics).

String a bicone. With the largest part of your roundnose pliers, make the first half of a wrapped loop.

3 Attach the crystal units to the wrapped loop. Complete the wraps.

4 Open the loop of an earring wire (Basics). Attach the dangle and close the loop. Make a second earring to match the first. ❖

DESIGN OPTION
Replace the crystal strand with a silver chain to draw more attention to the sparkling centerpiece.

Mon

WireLace provides a
flexible landscape for
a pastel palette

et's colors bloom
in a crystal necklace

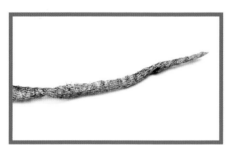

1 Cut a 1-yd. (.9m) piece of WireLace. (My necklace is 17 in./43cm.) Twist each end. Trim the ends at an angle to form a tip, and apply epoxy to each tip.

2 Center an octagonal crystal on the WireLace.

3 a Cut a 30-in. (76cm) piece of beading wire. String the wire through the octagonal crystal, being careful not to snag the WireLace. Pull the wire through until one side is about 2 in. (5cm) longer than the other.

b On the longer side, string an alternating pattern of six top-drilled bicone crystals and five octagons. If you are using two colors of octagons, alternate colors.

4 String the beaded end of the wire through the centered octagon, forming a loop. String the wire through all the crystals and back through the centered octagon.

by Linda Hartung

Capture the colors of Monet's *Water Lilies* in this clever necklace with aqua, green, and lavender crystals paired with teal WireLace. Or, create your own garden with seasonal colors.

SUPPLY NOTES
- Use silver-plated beading wire — .018 or thinner — so it disappears in the focal piece and fits the center part of the flower.
- The thickness of the WireLace and the hole size of some crystals vary. When shopping for materials, make sure the WireLace will go through the crystals.

5 Adjust the wire so it's approximately the same length on both sides (within 2 in./5cm). Tighten the wire and arrange the crystals to form a flower. Tighten the wire again. String a crimp bead on each end and crimp the crimp beads (Basics, p. 12) as close to the crystal flower as possible.

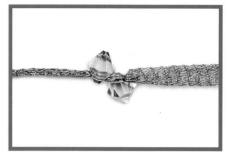

6 On each end of the WireLace, string pairs of bicones 1½ in. (3.8cm) apart until the strand is within 1 in. (2.5cm) of the desired length.

7 Gently pull the sides of the WireLace apart between each crystal pair and after the last pair.

SupplyList

For retail sites, contact AlaCarte Clasps, 800-977-2825, alacarteclasps.com.
- **6** 14mm octagonal crystals, in one or two colors
- **36–40** 6mm saucer crystals, top drilled
- **36–40** 6mm bicone crystals, top drilled
- **3g** 13º seed beads
- silver-plated flexible beading wire, .018
- **1** yd. (.9m) WireLace
- **2** 4mm bell end caps
- **4** 2mm crimp beads
- teardrop-shaped clasp
- **8** x 4.8mm teardrop-shaped crystal for clasp
- chainnose pliers
- diagonal wire cutters
- crimping pliers (optional)
- 2-part epoxy

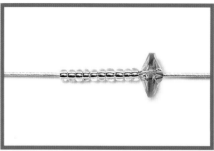

8 On each end of the wire, string ten 13º seed beads and a saucer crystal.

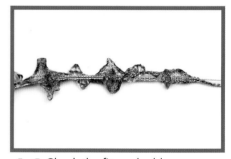

9 On each side, string each end of the wire through the first section of WireLace.

10 On each end of the wire, string a saucer, 20 13ºs, a saucer, and the next section of WireLace. Repeat until the wire has passed between the last set of crystal pairs.

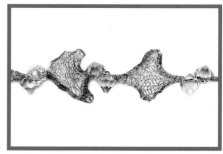

11 Check the fit, and add or remove beads if necessary. On each end of the wire, string a saucer and ten 13ºs. On each side, string a crimp bead over both the wire and the WireLace. Crimp the crimp bead (Basics).

12 Apply epoxy to the inside of an end cap, and attach it to one end of the strand. Repeat on the other end.

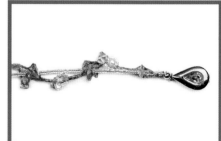

13 On each end, open the loop of the end cap and attach half a clasp. Glue the teardrop-shaped crystal to the clasp using epoxy. ❖

Shortcuts

Readers' tips to make your beading life easier

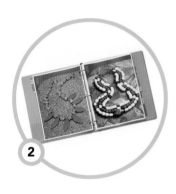

1 scarf hanger
A scarf hanger is a tangle-free way to store necklaces. This wooden hanger has ten large holes, so I can display 10 to 40 necklaces. The hanger shown here is available from stacksandstacks.com.
– *Cory Marchant, St. Paul, Minn.*

2 beading binder
I've amassed a number of beading magazines, but sticky notes poking out all over are unmanageable. So, I cut out what I wanted to keep and invested in a binder, dividers, and a box of clear plastic sheet inserts. I labeled the sections "necklaces," "bracelets," "earrings," and "Web sites and vendors." The binder keeps everything organized, so I can easily find what I'm looking for.
– *Nita Mentz, Franklin, Minn.*

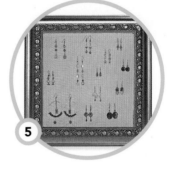

3 chalk it up
I place a broken piece of dustless chalk in a zip-top bag with my silver findings. The chalk absorbs moisture and prevents the silver from tarnishing.
– *Tia Torhorst, Washington, D.C.*

4 magnetic tool holder
During my last visit to a home-goods store, I purchased a magnetic knife holder for the wall of my work area. It conveniently holds my tools and keeps my work area clutter-free.
– *Christina Campagna, via e-mail*

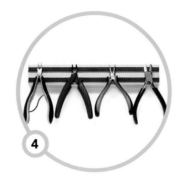

5 framed works of art
Using a staple gun, I attached fine mesh screening to the back of a picture frame. I hang earrings on the mesh so visitors to my studio can easily see them.
– *Carol J. Kelly, New Smyrna Beach, Fla.*

Mixed

materials

Make a button
BLOOM

Frame a button with interchangeable petal collars

by Julie Paasch-Anderson

A button blossoms when you surround it with a collar of petal-shaped beads. The collar keeps the button from flipping over, and it's interchangeable. So, you can mix and match colors or wear more than one at a time for a fuller bloom in this bracelet and earrings.

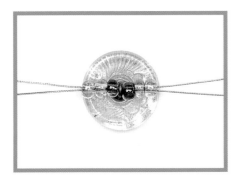

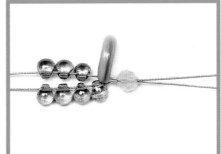

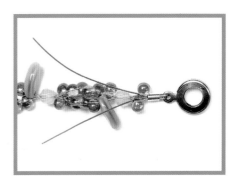

1 bracelet • Cut two pieces of beading wire (Basics, p. 12). Over both wires, center three or four 6º seed beads, a button, and three or four 6ºs.

2 On each end, on one wire, string three to five fringe beads and a leaf bead. On the other wire, string four to six fringe beads. Over both wires, string a 4mm round bead. Repeat until the strand is within 1 in. (2.5cm) of the finished length.

3 On each end, on each wire, string a fringe bead. Over both wires, string a crimp bead and half of a snap clasp. Check the fit, and add or remove beads from each end if necessary. Go back through the beads just strung and tighten the wire. Crimp the crimp bead (Basics) and trim the excess wire.

BRACELET OPTION #1

Use side-to-side–drilled leaf beads instead of the front-to-back–drilled leaves, and use 9mm flower beads instead of the 4mm round beads.

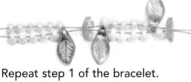

Repeat step 1 of the bracelet. String the pattern as shown. Repeat until the strand is within 1 in. (2.5cm) of the finished length. Repeat steps 3, 4, and 5.

BRACELET OPTION #2

Use 10mm cathedral fire-polished crystals instead of the leaves, and use 4mm flat spacers instead of the 4mm rounds.

Repeat step 1 of the bracelet. String the pattern as shown. Repeat until the strand is within 1 in. (2.5cm) of the finished length. Repeat steps 3, 4, and 5.

4 To make a petal collar: Cut a 3-in. (7.6cm) piece of elastic cord. String 10 to 14 16mm dagger beads. Tie a surgeon's knot (Basics). Trim the excess cord. If desired, make another petal collar with 10mm daggers.

5 To wear: Gently stretch one or two petal collars over the button.

1 **earrings •** Make a petal collar as in step 4 of the bracelet; do not trim the excess cord. Cut a 3-in. (7.6cm) piece of 22-gauge wire. Make a wrapped loop on one end (Basics, p. 12).

2 Lay the petal collar over the back of a button. String the wire through the shank of the button. Tie a surgeon's knot with the cord around the wire. Trim the excess cord.

3 Make a wrapped loop.

4 Open a jump ring (Basics). Attach a leaf bead and the bottom loop. Close the jump ring.

5 Open the loop of an earring wire (Basics). Attach the dangle and close the loop. Make a second earring to match the first. ❖

Supply**List**

bracelet
- 18–28mm button with shank
- **10–14** 16mm dagger beads
- **8–10** 10mm leaf beads, front-to-back drilled (The Glass Bead Garden, glassbeadgarden.com)
- **8–10** 4mm round beads
- 2g fringe beads
- **6–8** 6º seed beads
- **10–14** 10mm dagger beads (optional)
- flexible beading wire, .014 or .015
- elastic cord, 1mm diameter
- **2** crimp beads
- snap clasp
- chainnose or crimping pliers
- diagonal wire cutters

earrings
- **2** 18mm buttons with shanks
- **24** 16mm dagger beads
- **2** 10mm leaf beads, front-to-back drilled (The Glass Bead Garden)
- 6 in. (15cm) 22-gauge half-hard wire
- elastic cord, 1mm diameter
- **2** 4mm jump rings
- pair of decorative earring wires
- chainnose and roundnose pliers
- diagonal wire cutters

Prepare a feast of pearls with a multistrand necklace and drop earrings

by Teri Bienvenue

A nine-strand necklace is a
BEAD BANQUET

When served together, a multitude of pearls, faceted rondelles, and seed beads is a savory complement to an engraved pendant. And for dessert, a pair of sweet earrings.

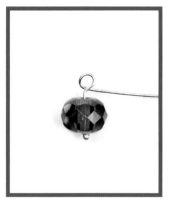

1 necklace • On a 1½-in. (3.8cm) decorative head pin, string a color A rondelle. Make the first half of a wrapped loop (Basics, p. 12). Repeat, making 24 to 30 color A rondelle units. Complete the wraps on half of the units, setting them aside for step 6.

2 Cut a 1½-in. (3.8cm) piece of chain. String two or three units on each link and complete the wraps.

3 To make a bail: Cut a 2-in. (5cm) piece of beading wire. String a pendant, approximately 1¼ in. (3.2cm) of 11º seed beads, and a crimp bead. Go back through the 11ºs on each side of the crimp bead. Crimp the crimp bead (Basics) and trim the excess wire.

4 On a 2-in. (5cm) head pin, string a color A rondelle and the pendant. Make the first half of a wrapped loop, attach the chain, and complete the wraps.

Cut eight pieces of beading wire (Basics). Cut another piece 4 in. (10cm) longer. (The longest strand of each of my necklaces is 19 in./48cm.)

5 On the first wire, string: two 11ºs, color B rondelle, two 11ºs, three top-drilled pearls, two 11ºs, potato-shaped pearl, two 11ºs, three top-drilled pearls.

On the second wire, string: two 11ºs, three top-drilled pearls, two 11ºs, 6mm round crystal, two 11ºs, three top-drilled pearls, two 11ºs, bicone crystal.

On the longest (third) wire, center the pendant.

On each end of the longest wire, string: two 11ºs, three top-drilled pearls, two 11ºs, round pearl, two 11ºs, three top-drilled pearls, two 11ºs, bicone, 11º.

Repeat each pattern on the respective wire until each strand is within 2 in. (5cm) of the desired length.

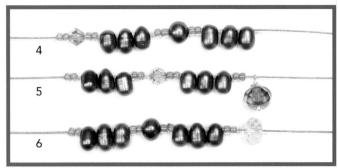

6 On the fourth wire, string: two 11ºs, bicone, two 11ºs, three top-drilled pearls, two 11ºs, round pearl, two 11ºs, three top-drilled pearls.

On the fifth wire, string: two 11ºs, three top-drilled pearls, two 11ºs, 4mm round crystal, two 11ºs, three top-drilled pearls, two 11ºs, rondelle unit.

On the sixth wire, string: two 11ºs, three top-drilled pearls, two 11ºs, round pearl, two 11ºs, three top-drilled pearls, two 11ºs, color C rondelle.

Repeat each pattern on the respective wire until each strand is within 2 in. (5cm) of the desired length.

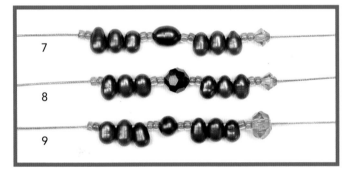

7 On the seventh wire, string: two 11ºs, three top-drilled pearls, two 11ºs, potato pearl, two 11ºs, three top-drilled pearls, two 11ºs, bicone.

On the eighth wire, string: two 11ºs, three top-drilled pearls, two 11ºs, 6mm round, two 11ºs, three top-drilled pearls, two 11ºs, bicone.

On the ninth wire, string: two 11ºs, three top-drilled pearls, two 11ºs, round pearl, two 11ºs, three top-drilled pearls, two 11ºs, color D rondelle.

Repeat each pattern on the respective wire until each strand is within 2 in. (5cm) of the desired length.

8 On each end of the first three wires, string three 11ºs, a crimp bead, and a spacer. String the wires through the bottom loop of half of a box clasp. Check the fit, and add or remove beads if necessary. Go back through the beads just strung and tighten the wires. Crimp the crimp beads and trim the excess wire.

Repeat, stringing the fourth, fifth, and sixth wires through the middle loop of the box clasp and the remaining wires through the top loop of the box clasp.

SupplyList

necklace
- 45 x 54mm teardrop-shaped pendant with 14mm hole (Lillypilly Designs, lillypillydesigns.com)
- 16-in. (41cm) strand 6mm potato-shaped pearls
- 5 16-in. (41cm) strands 4–5mm pearls, top drilled
- 16-in. (41cm) strand 4mm round pearls

- 4 16-in. (41cm) strands 6mm faceted rondelles, in four colors
- 18–26 6mm round crystals
- 10–14 4mm round crystals
- 46–66 4mm bicone crystals
- 24g 11º seed beads
- 18 3mm spacers
- flexible beading wire, .014 or .015
- 1½ in. (3.8cm) chain, 4–5mm links
- 2-in. (5cm) head pin

- 24–30 1½-in. (3.8cm) decorative head pins
- 19 crimp beads
- three-strand box clasp
- chainnose and roundnose pliers
- diagonal wire cutters
- crimping pliers (optional)

earrings
- 2 23 x 26mm teardrop-shaped pendants (Lillypilly Designs, lillypillydesigns.com)

- 2 6mm potato-shaped pearls
- 2 6mm faceted rondelles
- 2 4mm spacers
- 4 in. (10cm) 24-gauge half-hard wire
- pair of earring wires
- chainnose and roundnose pliers
- diagonal wire cutters

EDITOR'S TIP
To simplify the necklace stringing, repeat the same pearl-and-crystal pattern on several strands.

1 **earrings** • Cut a 2-in. (5cm) piece of wire. Make the first half of a wrapped loop (Basics, p. 12), and string a pendant. Complete the wraps.

2 String a rondelle, a spacer, and a potato-shaped pearl. Make a wrapped loop.

3 Open the loop of an earring wire (Basics) and attach the dangle. Close the loop. Make a second earring to match the first. ❖

String an

eclectic
mix

Design an unusual necklace and earrings with an assortment of beads

by Heather Powers

This necklace has it all — an art bead, gemstones, pearls, seed beads, and a metal pendant. It even has a button to play up its handcrafted appeal. The combination of single and double strands highlights the necklace's asymmetry, and colorful drop earrings make an unfussy accompaniment.

1 **necklace** • Cut two pieces of beading wire (Basics, p. 12). (The dragonfly necklace is 18 in./46cm; the leaf necklace, 19 in./48cm.) Center a pendant over both wires.

2 On one end, over both wires, string an 8mm round bead, a 5mm bead, and a button.

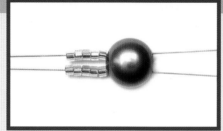

3 On the other end, over both wires, string: two 8mm rounds, large spacer, tube bead, large spacer, 9–10mm bead, small spacer.

4 On the side with the tube, separate the wires. On each end, string five 11º Japanese cylinder beads and the corresponding holes of a double-drilled pearl. Repeat five times, then string five cylinder beads.

5 On the same side, over both wires, string: small spacer, 9–10mm bead, large spacer, 9–10mm bead. String an 8mm round and a small spacer, repeating until the strand is within 1 in. (2.5cm) of half of the finished length. End with an 8mm round.

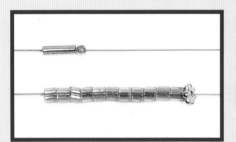

6 On the side with the button, separate the wires. On one end, string a bugle bead and an 11º seed bead.

On the other end, string 11 8º hex-cut seed beads and a small spacer.

Repeat the respective patterns until the strands are within 1 in. (2.5cm) of the finished length.

7 On each end, over both wires, string: small spacer, 6mm crystal, crimp bead, 8º, half of a clasp. Check the fit, and add or remove beads if necessary. Go back through the beads just strung and tighten the wires. Crimp the crimp bead (Basics) and trim the excess wire.

···

Supply List

necklace
- 50–55mm tube-shaped art bead (Heather Powers, humblebeads.com)
- 35–45mm pendant
- 17–19mm button with shank
- **3** 9–10mm accent beads
- **6** 8mm double-drilled pearls (Eclectica, 262-641-0910)
- **6–9** 8mm round beads
- **2** 6mm crystals
- 5mm bead
- 2g size 2 (6mm) bugle beads
- 5g 8º hex-cut seed beads
- 1g 11º Japanese cylinder beads
- 1g 11º seed beads
- **3** 8–9mm (large) spacers
- **13–20** 3mm (small) flat spacers
- flexible beading wire, .010 or .012
- **2** crimp beads
- toggle clasp
- chainnose or crimping pliers
- diagonal wire cutters

earrings
- **2** 9–10mm accent beads
- **4** 8mm round beads
- **4** 3mm flat spacers
- **2** 1½-in. (3.8cm) head pins with paddles
- pair of earring posts with ear nuts
- chainnose and roundnose pliers
- diagonal wire cutters

1 earrings • On a decorative head pin, string: 9–10mm bead, spacer, 8mm round bead, spacer, 8mm round. Make a plain loop (Basics, p. 12).

2 Open the loop of an earring post (Basics) and attach the dangle. Close the loop. Make a second earring to match the first. ❖

EDITOR'S TIP
Select the art bead first, then choose a button to complement it. Once you've chosen these key elements, it will be easy to find a pendant that works with them.

Keep an
artistic
focus

Show off art beads
with a simply strung
strand and earrings

by Ann Smith

You can highlight the dominant qualities of an art bead in the supporting strand by choosing beads with similar characteristics. Or, string a mix of similar and contrasting beads for a more intricate look.

1 necklace • Decide how long you want your necklace to be. (My necklaces are 16 in./41cm.) Add 10 in. (25cm) and cut a piece of beading wire to that length. Center a teardrop crystal on the wire.

2 Over both ends of the wire, string an art bead and a 6mm bead.

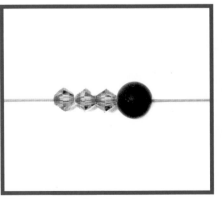

3 On each end, string three bicone crystals and a 6mm. Repeat three times.

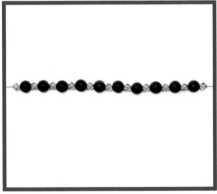

4 Cut a 20-in. (51cm) piece of beading wire. String an alternating pattern of 11 bicones and ten 6mms.

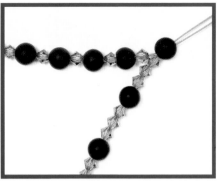

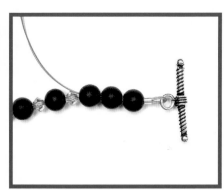

5 String each end of the 20-in. (51cm) wire through an end bead of the other strand.

On each end, over both wires, string an alternating pattern of bicones and 6mms until the strand is within 3 in. (7.6cm) of the finished length.

6 On each end, over both wires, string three 6mms, a crimp bead, and half of a clasp. Check the fit, and add or remove beads from each end if necessary. Go back through the beads just strung and tighten the wires. Crimp the crimp beads (Basics, p. 12) and trim the excess wire.

1 earrings • On a head pin, string a bicone crystal, a barrel-shaped art bead, and a bicone. Make a wrapped loop (Basics, p. 12).

2 Open the loop of an earring wire (Basics). Attach the dangle and close the loop. Make a second earring to match the first ❧

Supply List

necklace
- 36–50mm tube-shaped art bead
- 11 x 5.5mm teardrop crystal
- **43–47** 6mm round or oval beads
- **55–59** 4mm bicone crystals
- flexible beading wire, .014 or .015
- **2** crimp beads
- toggle clasp
- chainnose or crimping pliers
- diagonal wire cutters

earrings
- **2** 12 x 15mm barrel-shaped art beads
- **4** 4mm bicone crystals
- **2** 2-in. (5cm) head pins
- pair of earring wires
- chainnose and roundnose pliers
- diagonal wire cutters

SUPPLY NOTES
- The glass art bead is available from Heiden & Engle Studios, 978-928-5495, heiden-engle.com.
- The etched glass art bead is available from Turtle Moon Arts, turtlemoonarts.com.
- The silk art bead is available from Kristal Wick Creations, 866-811-1376, kristalwick.com.

DESIGN OPTIONS
- If you're using a matte art bead, substitute 4mm matte beads for the crystals.
- Eliminating the joining strand creates a more casual design.

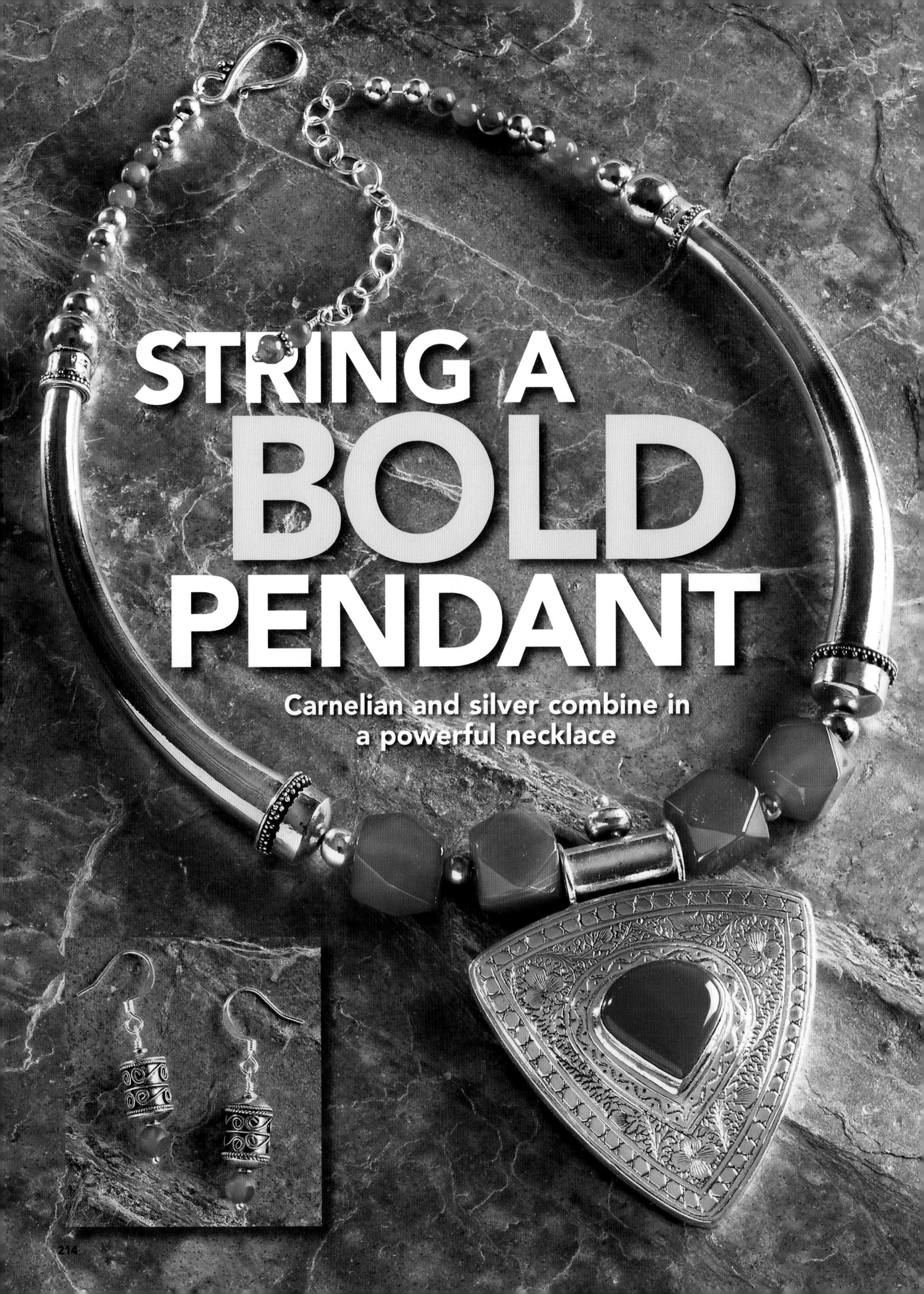

STRING A
BOLD
PENDANT

Carnelian and silver combine in a powerful necklace

by Rupa Balachandar

A shield-shaped pendant, carnelian nuggets, and dramatic silver tubes come together in a simple yet striking necklace. Not for the faint of heart, this necklace complements a fierce style. The best part is, you can make the necklace and earrings in less than half an hour for fantastic results without a heroic effort.

1 earrings • On a head pin, string a carnelian bead and a silver bead. Make a wrapped loop (Basics, p. 12).

2 Open the loop of an earring wire (Basics). Attach the dangle and close the loop. Make a second earring to match the first. ❖

1 necklace • Cut a piece of beading wire (Basics, p. 12). (My necklace is 17½ in./44.5cm.) Center a pendant on the wire.

2 On each end, string a nugget, a 5mm silver bead, a nugget, and a 7mm silver bead.

3 On each end, string the three parts of a curved tube bead.

4 On each end, string a 7mm silver bead, two carnelian beads, and two 5mm silver beads. String carnelian beads until the strand is within 2 in. (5cm) of the desired length.

5 On one end, string a 5mm silver bead, a crimp bead, a 5mm silver bead, and a hook clasp. Repeat on the other end, substituting a 3-in. (7.6cm) piece of chain for the clasp. Check the fit, and add or remove beads from each end if necessary. Go back through the beads just strung and tighten the wire. Crimp the crimp beads (Basics) and trim the excess wire.

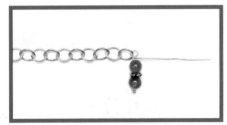

6 On a decorative head pin, string a carnelian bead, a flat spacer, and a carnelian bead. Make the first half of a wrapped loop (Basics). Attach the dangle to the end of the chain and complete the wraps.

SupplyList

necklace
- triangular silver pendant, approximately 60 x 70mm (Rupa B. Designs, rupab.com)
- **2** 4½-in. (11.4cm) curved tube beads (Rupa B. Designs)
- **4** 14–16mm faceted carnelian nuggets
- **10–18** 5mm round carnelian beads
- **4** 7mm round silver beads
- **10** 5mm round silver beads
- 5mm flat spacer
- flexible beading wire, .018 or .019
- 2-in. (5cm) decorative head pin
- **2** crimp beads
- hook clasp
- 3 in. (7.6cm) chain for extender, 5–6mm links
- chainnose and roundnose pliers
- diagonal wire cutters
- crimping pliers (optional)

earrings
- **2** 10–15mm silver beads
- **2** 5mm round carnelian beads
- **2** 2-in. (5cm) decorative head pins
- pair of earring wires
- chainnose and roundnose pliers
- diagonal wire cutters

Clover accents

Make a simple embellishment for a beaded pendant

by Tammy Powley

An easy wire clover made of three simple loops adds distinction to a classic necklace and is the perfect setting for a gemstone nugget or an art bead. Carry the theme to the earrings with smaller clovers.

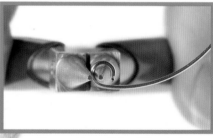

1 **necklace** • Cut a 5-in. (13cm) piece of 24-gauge wire. Using roundnose pliers, make a loop on one end. For a 4mm loop, wrap the wire about ½ in. (1.3cm) from the pliers' tip.

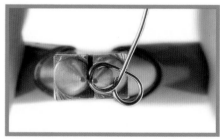

2 Position the pliers next to the first loop. Make a second loop.

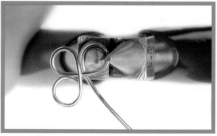

3 Repeat step 2 next to the second loop.

4 String a bicone crystal, a focal bead, and a bicone. Make a wrapped loop (Basics, p. 12) perpendicular to the clover.

5 Cut a piece of beading wire (Basics, p. 12) (My necklaces are 19 in./48cm.) On the wire, center: 2mm spacer, cube crystal, 2mm spacer, pearl, flat spacer, pearl, focal-bead unit, pearl, flat spacer, pearl, 2mm spacer, cube, 2mm spacer.

6 On each end, string: pearl, flat spacer, pearl, flat spacer, pearl, bicone, nugget or rondelle, bicone.

7 On each end, string: pearl, flat spacer, pearl, flat spacer, pearl, 2mm spacer, cube, 2mm spacer.

8 Repeat step 6 until the strand is within 1 in. (2.5cm) of the desired length. On one end, string a bicone, a crimp bead, a bicone, and a lobster claw clasp. Go back through the beads just strung and tighten the wire. Repeat on the other end, substituting a soldered jump ring for the clasp. Check the fit, and add or remove beads from each end if necessary. Crimp the crimp beads (Basics) and trim the excess wire.

Supply List

necklace
- 20–40mm focal bead (lampworked bead by Lisa Kan, lisakan.com)
- **10–14** 8mm gemstone nuggets or rondelles
- **4** 8mm cube crystals
- 16-in. (41cm) strand 7mm button pearls
- **26–30** 4mm bicone crystals
- **32–36** 4mm flat spacers
- **8** 2mm spacers
- flexible beading wire, .014 or .015
- 5 in. (13cm) 24-gauge half-hard wire
- **2** crimp beads

- lobster claw clasp and soldered jump ring
- chainnose and roundnose pliers
- diagonal wire cutters
- crimping pliers (optional)

earrings
- **2** 8mm gemstone nuggets or rondelles
- **4** 4mm bicone crystals
- **4** 4mm flat spacers
- 4 in. (10cm) 24-gauge half-hard wire
- pair of earring wires
- chainnose and roundnose pliers
- diagonal wire cutters

1 earrings • Cut a 2-in. (5cm) piece of 24-gauge wire. Follow steps 1–3 of the necklace, using the tip of your roundnose pliers to make smaller loops.

2 String: bicone crystal, flat spacer, nugget or rondelle, flat spacer, bicone. Make a wrapped loop (Basics, p. 12).

3 Open the loop of an earring wire (Basics). Attach the dangle and close the loop. Make a second earring to match the first. ❖

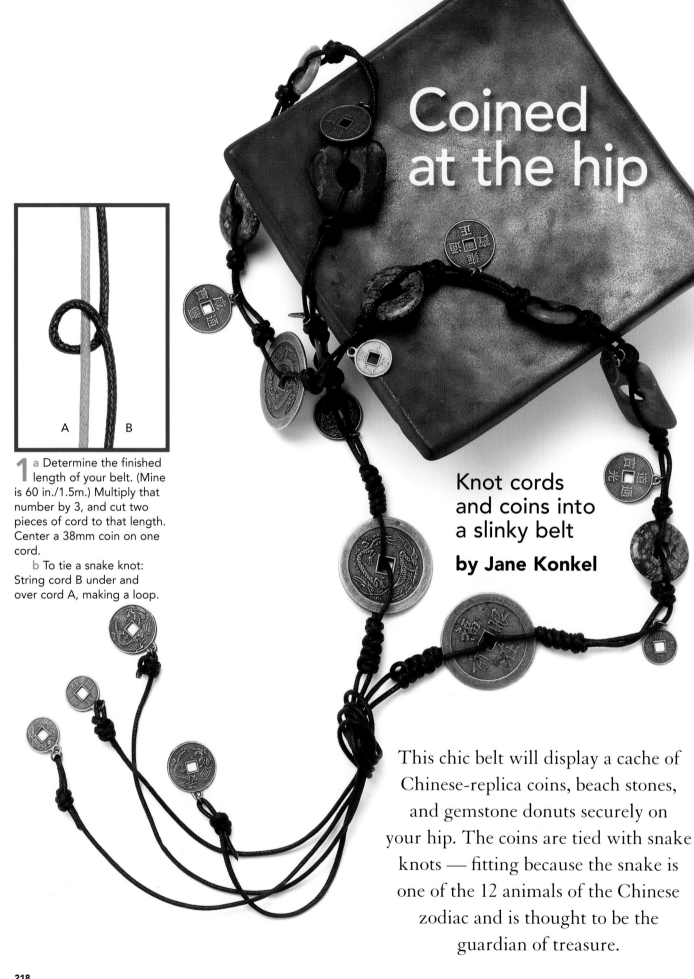

Coined at the hip

Knot cords and coins into a slinky belt

by Jane Konkel

1 a Determine the finished length of your belt. (Mine is 60 in./1.5m.) Multiply that number by 3, and cut two pieces of cord to that length. Center a 38mm coin on one cord.

b To tie a snake knot: String cord B under and over cord A, making a loop.

A   B

This chic belt will display a cache of Chinese-replica coins, beach stones, and gemstone donuts securely on your hip. The coins are tied with snake knots — fitting because the snake is one of the 12 animals of the Chinese zodiac and is thought to be the guardian of treasure.

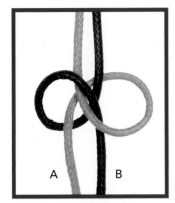

A B

2 String A over B and through the first loop, making a loop with A. Pull both ends to loosely close the knot.

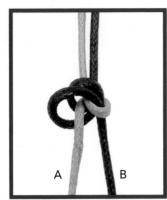

A B

3 String B under A and down through A's loop. Pull B to loosely close the knot.

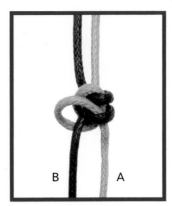

B A

4 Turn the cords over. String A under B and down through the lower of the two loops. Pull cord A to loosely close the knot.

5 Turn the cords over. Approximately 1 in. (2.5cm) from the knot, tie a snake knot. String a donut, crossing each end through the center.
Tie a snake knot.

6 Continue stringing donuts and 38mm coins and tying snake knots until the knotted section is within 2 in. (5cm) of half the desired length.
Approximately 1 in. (2.5cm) from the last knot, tie a snake knot. Turn the cords over, and repeat steps 3 and 4 four times. String a 38mm coin.

7 Tie a snake knot. Turn the cords over, and repeat steps 3 and 4 four times.

8 Open a jump ring (Basics, p. 12) and attach a single-loop coin. Close the jump ring. On the end of one cord, string the coin, leaving a 2-in. (5cm) tail. Tie an overhand knot (Basics). Trim the excess cord. Repeat with the remaining cord.

9 To finish the other half of the belt: Center the 38mm coin (from step 1) on the second cord. Repeat steps 1b–8. Use jump rings to attach single-loop coins to the cord between knots. ❖

Supply List

- **3–5** 38mm coins, center drilled (all coins from Fire Mountain Gems, 800-355-2137, firemountaingems.com)
- **2–4** beach-stone donuts, approximately 35mm (Riverstone Bead Company, 219-939-2050, riverstonebead.com)
- **6–8** 20–30mm gemstone donuts, in two sizes
- **14–18** 15–20mm single-loop coins, in two sizes
- **14–18** 5mm inside diameter antique-gold jump rings
- **9–11** ft. (2.7–3.4m) 2mm woven cord
- chainnose and roundnose pliers or **2** pairs of chainnose pliers
- diagonal wire cutters

EDITOR'S TIPS
- To distinguish cord A from cord B, the photos in steps 1–4 show cords in different colors.
- Learn how to tie a snake knot and other decorative Chinese knots in Suzen Millodot's *Chinese Knots for Beaded Jewellery*.

CULTIVATE A

Plant a Celtic cross in a verdant setting

by Cathy Jakicic

Combine peridot, green quartz, and coppery tones with silk ribbons to provide a lush backdrop for a Celtic cross. The range of textures adds depth to the necklace and the cluster earrings, which carry on the earthy theme.

FIELD OF GREEN

1 **necklace** • Fold two ribbons in half and string the ends through a pendant. Pull the ends through the resulting loop.

2 Cut a piece of beading wire (Basics, p. 12). (My necklace is 19 in./48cm.) Center the knot on the wire.

3 On each end of one ribbon, starting 1 in. (2.5cm) from the pendant, tie an overhand knot (Basics). String a large-hole bead and tie an overhand knot. String another large-hole bead and tie an overhand knot. Repeat the sequence twice, spacing each group 3–4 in. (7.6–10cm) apart.

4 On each end of the second ribbon, starting 2 in. (5cm) from the pendant, tie an overhand knot. String a large-hole bead and tie an overhand knot. Repeat the sequence twice, spacing each bead 3–4 in. (7.6–10cm) apart.

Supply List

necklace
- Celtic cross pendant, approximately 25 x 50mm (Clay River Designs, 303-849-5234, clayriverdesigns.com)
- **20–24** 8mm faceted round beads
- **16–22** 8mm large-hole round beads
- 16-in. (41cm) strand 3 x 6mm teardrop-shaped beads, top drilled
- flexible beading wire, .014 or .015
- **2** 42-in. (1.1m) dyed silk ribbons, in two colors (Silk Painting is Fun, 928-607-2765, silkpaintingisfun.com)
- 8 in. (20cm) 20-gauge half-hard wire

- **2** crimp beads
- **2** cones, approximately 25mm
- lobster claw clasp
- chainnose and roundnose pliers
- diagonal wire cutters
- crimping pliers (optional)

earrings
- **2** 8mm faceted round beads
- **12** 3 x 6mm teardrop-shaped beads, top drilled
- flexible beading wire, .014 or .015
- **2** crimp beads
- pair of earring wires
- chainnose or crimping pliers
- diagonal wire cutters

5 On each end of the beading wire, string 11 teardrop-shaped beads and two faceted beads. Repeat until the strand is within 3 in. (7.6cm) of the finished length.

6 Cut two 4-in. (10cm) pieces of 20-gauge wire and make a wrapped loop (Basics) on one end of each.

On one end of the beading wire, string a crimp bead and a wrapped loop. Check the fit, allowing 2 in. (5cm) for finishing. Add or remove beads, if necessary. Go back through the last few beads strung and crimp the crimp bead (Basics). Trim the excess wire. Repeat on the other end.

7 On each side, string the ends of both ribbons through the wrapped loop and tie a surgeon's knot (Basics). Trim the ends of the ribbon ½ in. (1.3cm) from the knot.

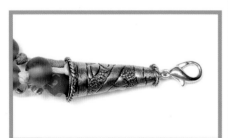

8 On one end, string a cone over the wire and make the first half of a wrapped loop. Attach a lobster claw clasp and complete the wraps. Repeat on the other end, omitting the clasp.

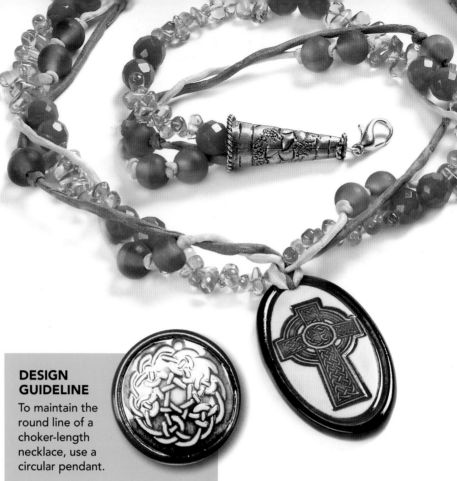

DESIGN GUIDELINE
To maintain the round line of a choker-length necklace, use a circular pendant.

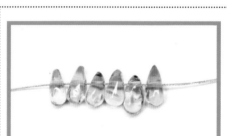

1 **earrings •** Cut a 5-in. (13cm) piece of beading wire. Center six teardrop-shaped beads on the wire.

2 String a faceted bead over both ends of the wire.

3 Over both ends, string a crimp bead and the loop of an earring wire. Go back through the crimp bead and the faceted bead. Crimp the crimp bead (Basics, p. 12). Trim the excess wire. Make a second earring to match the first. ❖

How can I finish cord without a clasp?

Wear the slide in the front or the back of the necklace.

by Linda Osterhoudt

A large-hole bead can be a clever substitute for a clasp on a suede lariat. This version features long cords in two colors and a bail wrapped with twisted wire. Crystals dress up this otherwise organic piece.

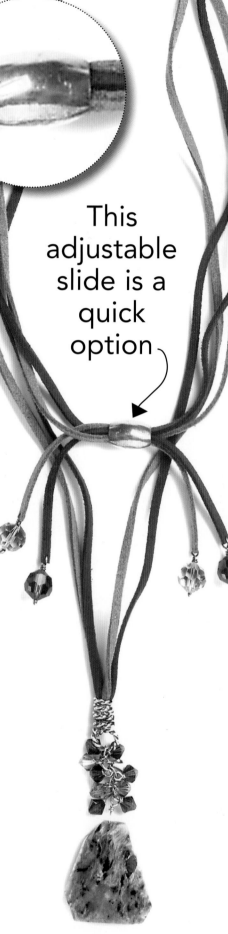

This adjustable slide is a quick option

1 On a 2½-in. (6.4cm) head pin, string a pendant. (If the pendant's hole is large, string a spacer first.) Make the first half of a wrapped loop (Basics, p. 12).

2 Cut a ¾-in. (1.9cm) piece of chain. Attach the pendant's loop to the chain and complete the wraps.

3 On a 1½-in. (3.8cm) head pin, string a crystal. Make the first half of a wrapped loop. Repeat with the remaining crystals. Set the round-crystal units aside for step 9.

4 Attach two bicone-crystal units to each link and complete the wraps.

SUPPLY NOTE
Choose a metal bead with a hole large enough to accommodate four 3mm suede cords.

5 Cut a 10-in. (25cm) piece of twisted wire. Make the first half of a wrapped loop. Attach the dangle and complete the wraps.

6 Decide how long you want your lariat to be. (My lariats are 44 in./1.1m.) Cut two pieces of suede cord to that length.

Cut a 4-in. (10cm) piece of 20-gauge wire. Make a wrapped loop. Center the loop over both cords. Fold the cords in half and wrap the wire around both cords. Trim the excess wire.

7 Wrap the twisted wire around the 20-gauge wire wraps. Trim the excess wire and tuck the wire tail.

8 String each pair of cords through a large-hole bead in opposite directions. Check the fit, and trim the cords if necessary.

9 Using a thumbtack, pierce a hole approximately ⅛ in. (3mm) from each end of each cord. String a round-crystal unit through each pierced hole, and complete the wraps. ❖

SupplyList

- gemstone pendant, approximately 30mm
- **4** 8mm round crystals, in two colors
- **10–14** 6mm bicone crystals, in two colors
- large-hole metal bead
- 4mm spacer (optional)
- **2** 40–48-in. (1–1.2m) pieces 3mm suede cord
- 4 in. (10cm) 20-gauge half-hard wire
- 10 in. (25cm) 18- or 20-gauge twisted wire
- ¾ in. (1.9cm) chain, 3–4mm links
- 2½-in. (6.4cm) head pin or decorative head pin
- **14–18** 1½-in. (3.8cm) head pins or decorative head pins
- chainnose and roundnose pliers
- diagonal wire cutters
- thumbtack

Indulge your
fun side

Be seriously fashionable without taking yourself too seriously. Choose a pewter pendant that matches your personality, and accent it with thematically related beads and unusual yarn. Keep the whimsical mood going with a pair of matching earrings.

SUPPLY NOTES

- The pendants, the bee clasp, and the bee accent beads: Green Girl Studios, 828-298-2263, greengirlstudios.com.
- The glass flower beads and the flower clasp: Fusion Beads, 888-781-3559, fusionbeads.com.
- The fish toggle clasp: Fire Mountain Gems, 800-355-2137, firemountaingems.com.
- The brown-and-orange lampworked saucer beads: Grace Lampwork Beads and Jewelry, 408-806-1788, gracebeads.com.
- The lampworked shell and blue saucer beads: Becklin Bead Designs, becky@becklinbeaddesigns.com, becklinbeaddesigns.com.
- The novelty yarns: Jo-Ann Stores, joann.com.

1 necklace • Cut a piece of beading wire (Basics, p. 12). (The mermaid necklace is 18 in./46cm; the bee and monkey necklaces, 22 in./56cm.) On the wire, center: cylinder bead, 5–6mm spacer, pendant, 5–6mm spacer, cylinder.

2 On each end, string: three leaf-shaped beads, five cylinders, three leaves, two cylinders, flat spacer, saucer bead, flat spacer.

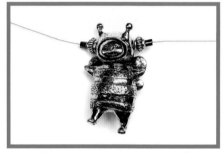

3 On each end, string two cylinders, three leaves, and an accent bead.

4 On each end, string: three leaves, two cylinders, flat spacer, saucer, flat spacer.

Create a
colorful habitat
for pewter pendants
with mixed media

by **Trish Kirkham**

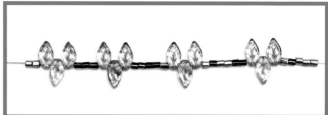

5 On each end, string: two cylinders, three leaves, three cylinders, three leaves, five cylinders, three leaves, six cylinders, three leaves, five cylinders. Repeat until the strand is within 1 in. (2.5cm) of the desired length.

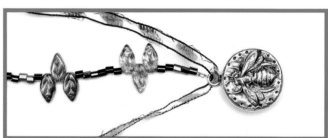

6 On each end, string a crimp bead and half of a clasp. Check the fit, and add or remove beads if necessary. Go back through the last few beads strung and tighten the wire. Crimp the crimp bead (Basics) and trim the excess wire.

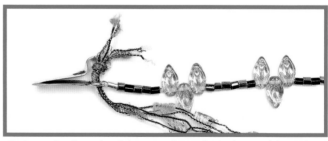

7 Double the desired length of your necklace, add 6 in. (15cm), and cut a piece of yarn to that length. On the yarn, center the loop of half of the clasp.

8 String both ends of the yarn through the loop of the other half of the clasp. Tie an overhand knot (Basics) with both strands. Trim the excess yarn, leaving ½-in. (1.3cm) tails.

Supply List

necklace
- pendant
- **2** 15–25mm accent beads
- **4** 15–18mm lampworked saucer beads
- **48–60** top-drilled leaf-shaped beads, approximately 5 x 10mm
- 3g 8º cylinder beads
- **2** 5–6mm spacers
- **8** 3–4mm flat spacers
- flexible beading wire, .014 or .0
- 42–50 in. (1.1–1.3m) novelty yar
- **2** crimp beads

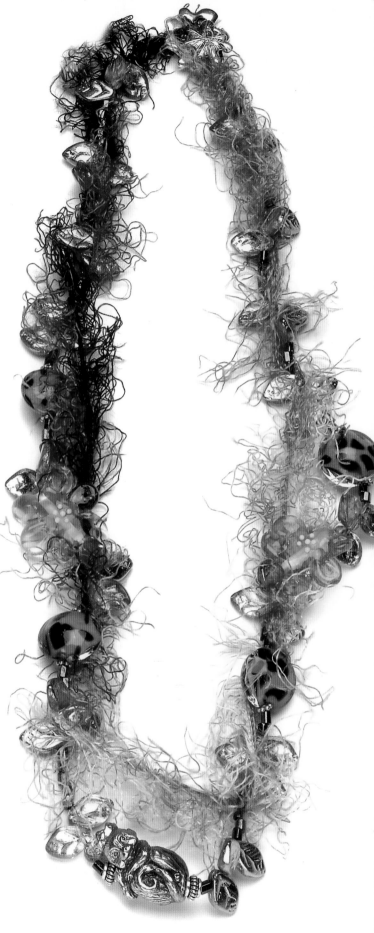

1 earrings • On a 2-in. (5cm) decorative head pin, string: cylinder bead, accent bead, cylinder, flat spacer, cylinder. Make a wrapped loop (Basics, p. 12).

2 Cut a 4-in. (10cm) piece of yarn. String both ends through another accent bead, leaving a loop above the bead. Tie an overhand knot (Basics). Trim the ends close to the knot.

3 Open the loop of an earring wire (Basics). Attach the dangles. Close the loop. Make a second earring to match the first. ❖

- clasp
- chainnose or crimping pliers
- diagonal wire cutters

earrings
- **4** 15–25mm accent beads
- **6** 8º cylinder beads
- **2** 3–4mm flat spacers

- 8–10 in. (20–25cm) novelty yarn
- **2** 2-in. (5cm) decorative head pins
- pair of earring wires
- chainnose and roundnose pliers
- diagonal wire cutters

Simple wreath
ornaments
brighten
holiday trees
or gifts

If you want a wreath design that's more you and less yuletide, string whatever combination you like — just make sure the beads have holes large enough to accommodate the memory wire.

by Naomi Fujimoto

Decorate with

1 On a head pin, string a 3mm bead. Make a wrapped loop (Basics, p. 12). Repeat with a 5mm bead. Make six 3mm-bead units and three 5mm-bead units.

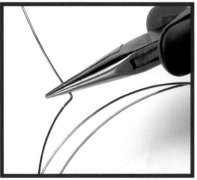

2 Separate one-and-a-half coils of memory wire from a stack of coils. Hold the wire with chainnose pliers and bend it back and forth at one place until the wire breaks. You also can use heavy-duty wire cutters. Do not use jewelry-weight wire cutters.

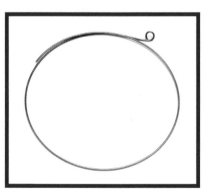

3 Using roundnose pliers, make a small loop on one end of the memory wire.

beaded wreaths

4 String a 6º seed bead and an 18mm round bead. Repeat seven times, substituting a cluster (two 3mm units and one 5mm unit) for the 6º three times. End with a 6º.

5 Trim the wire to ½ in. (1.3cm) and make a loop next to the last bead.

6 Cut a 12-in. (30cm) piece of ribbon. String it through both loops and tie a bow. Cut a 5-in. (13cm) piece of beading wire. String it through both loops. String both ends through a crimp bead and crimp the crimp bead (Basics). Trim the excess ribbon and wire. ❖

Flaunt a chain-link pendant

Frame a bold centerpiece with gemstones

by Rupa Balachandar

Using a detailed focal piece that requires minimal enhancement is a beautiful shortcut to a striking necklace. A single strand of faceted rondelles adds color while leaving the pendant in the spotlight.

1 necklace • Determine the finished length of your necklace. (Mine is 17 in./43cm.) Add 8 in. (20cm) and cut a piece of beading wire to that length. Cut the wire in half.

On each wire, string a crimp bead, a 4mm spacer, and a loop of a pendant. Go back through the beads just strung and tighten the wire. Crimp the crimp bead (Basics, p. 12). If desired, close a crimp cover over the crimp bead.

2 On each end, string five rondelles and a 6–7mm spacer. Repeat until the strand is within 1 in. (2.5cm) of the desired length. End with a rondelle.

3 On each end, string: 5mm spacer, accent bead, crimp bead, 5mm spacer, half of a clasp. Go back through the last few beads strung and tighten the wire. Check the fit, and add or remove beads from each end if necessary. Crimp the crimp bead and trim the excess wire. If desired, close a crimp cover over the crimp bead.

Supply List

necklace
- 2.5 x 10cm chain-link pendant (Rupa B. Designs, rupab.com)
- 16-in. (41cm) strand 10–12mm gemstone rondelles
- **2** 6–7mm accent beads
- **8–12** 6–7mm spacers
- **4** 5mm spacers
- **2** 4mm spacers
- flexible beading wire, .018 or .019
- **4** crimp beads
- **4** crimp covers (optional)
- toggle clasp
- chainnose or crimping pliers
- diagonal wire cutters

earrings
- **4** 6–8mm gemstone rondelles
- **2** 5–6mm spacers
- **2** 1½-in. (3.8cm) head pins
- pair of earring wires
- chainnose and roundnose pliers
- diagonal wire cutters

1 earrings • On a head pin, string a rondelle, a spacer, and a rondelle. Make a wrapped loop (Basics, p. 12).

2 Open the loop of an earring wire (Basics) and attach the dangle. Close the loop. Make a second earring to match the first. ✤

A D-ring attached to a cabochon, pendant, button, or other found object creates a removable focal point for a multistrand choker. You can quickly create a collection of these slides to move from casual to dressy in seconds. Take an extra ten minutes to make simple earrings that roll with the changes.

by Roxie Moede

Optimize a choker with multiple pendant options

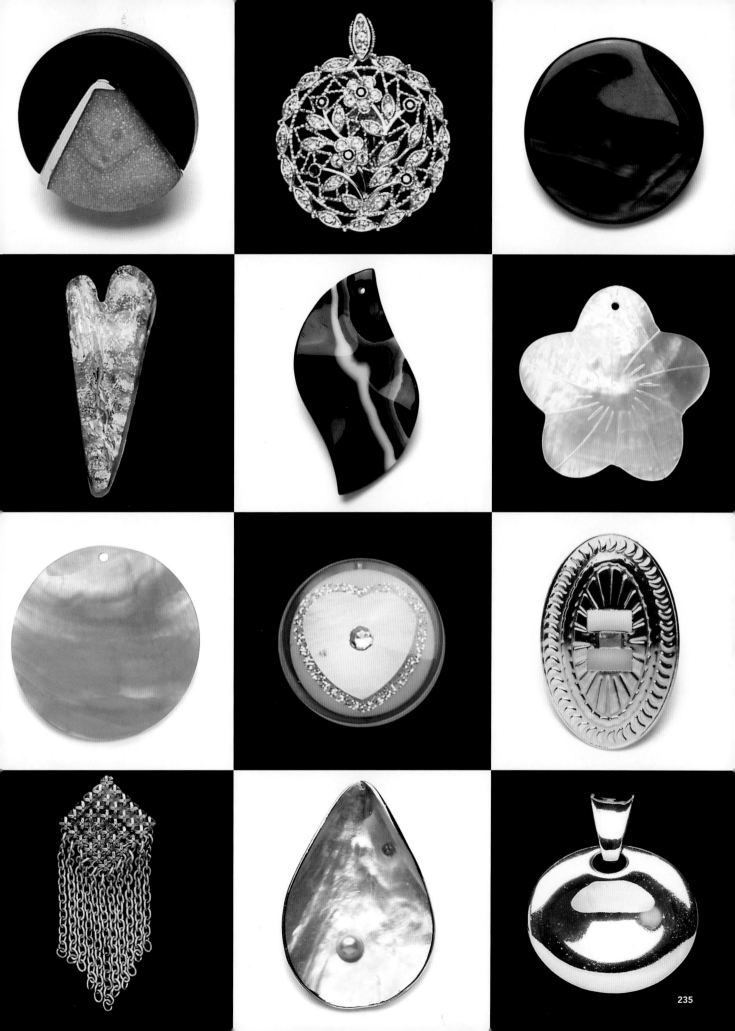

1 necklace • To make a pendant: Use glue to attach a D-ring to the back of a cabochon. Let it dry for 24 hours.

2 Cut two pieces of beading wire (Basics, p. 12). (My necklaces are 14 in./36cm.) Cut two more pieces: one ½ in. (1.3cm) longer than the original pieces and one ½ in. (1.3cm) shorter. On one wire, string 6º seed beads, interspersing 6mm round beads, until the strand is within 1 in. (2.5cm) of the desired length. Begin and end with a 6mm round.

3 On each of the remaining wires, string the pattern in step 2, positioning the 6mm rounds at different intervals on each strand.

EDITOR'S TIP
Choose a clasp that will fit through the D-ring.

4 On each end of each strand, string a 6º, a crimp bead, a 6º, and the corresponding loop of half of a clasp. Check the fit, and add or remove beads if necessary. Go back through the beads just strung and tighten the wires. Crimp the crimp bead (Basics) and trim the excess wire. Slide the pendant over the strands.

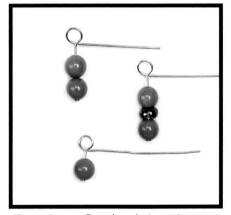

1 earrings • On a head pin, string two 6mm round beads. Make the first half of a wrapped loop (Basics, p. 12). On a second head pin, string a 6mm round. Make the first half of a wrapped loop. On a third head pin, string a 6mm round, a 6º seed bead, and a 6mm round. Make the first half of a wrapped loop.

2 Cut three 1-in. (2.5cm) pieces of chain. Attach a bead unit to each chain and complete the wraps.

3 Open the loop of an earring wire (Basics). Attach the dangles and close the loop. Make a second earring to match the first. ❖

Supply List

necklace
- 25 x 40mm cabochon (Fire Mountain Gems, 800-355-2137, firemountaingems.com)
- **48–60** 6mm round beads
- 20g 6º seed beads
- flexible beading wire, .014 or .015
- ¾-in. (1.9cm) D-ring (available at craft stores)
- **8** crimp beads

- clasp (orchid from Ayla's Originals, 877-328-2952, aylasoriginals.com)
- chainnose or crimping pliers
- diagonal wire cutters
- E6000 adhesive

earrings
- **10** 6mm round beads
- **2** 6º seed beads
- 7 in. (18cm) figaro chain
- **6** 1½-in. (3.8cm) head pins
- pair of earring wires
- chainnose and roundnose pliers
- diagonal wire cutters

A reversible
necklace turns
from casual to
dressy in a flash

Multitasking

Create jewelry as versatile as you — effortlessly elegant when the occasion arises and put-together even in the most casual setting. This necklace- and-earring set is perfect for a day with too many activities and too little time to switch gears.

For daytime, wear the leather side and casual pendant in front. Flip to the dressy pendant and the chain side for an evening out. Make the earrings a blend of both color schemes, and you'll weather any changes beautifully.

can be beautiful

by Jean Yates

SupplyList

pendant with jump ring bail
- 20–30mm focal bead
- **4** 4–5mm gemstone chips
- **2** 6–8mm flat spacers
- **2** 3–5mm flat spacers
- 3-in. (7.6cm) head pin
- **3** 10mm inside diameter jump rings
- chainnose and roundnose pliers
- diagonal wire cutters

pendant with chain dangles
- 20–30mm gemstone nugget
- 12mm cube crystal
- **2** 7–8mm potato-shaped pearls
- 7–8mm drop crystal
- 6mm round crystal
- **4** 4mm round crystals
- **5** 4mm spacers
- 4mm flat spacer
- **4** 8mm bead caps
- 12–14mm bail
- 3–4 in. (7.6–10cm) chain, 2–4mm links
- 3-in. (7.6cm) head pin
- **4** 2-in. (5cm) head pins
- 10mm inside diameter jump ring
- chainnose and roundnose pliers
- diagonal wire cutters

necklace
- 12-in. (30cm) triple-braided leather cord (The Bead Shop, 650-328-5291, beadshop.com)
- 20–26 in. (51–66cm) chain, 2–4mm links
- **2** 6mm inside diameter jump rings
- **2** 10mm crimp ends
- lobster claw clasp
- chainnose pliers
- diagonal wire cutters
- E6000 adhesive

earrings
- **2** 6mm round crystals
- **4** 4mm round crystals
- **4** 4–5mm gemstone chips
- **4** 4mm spacers
- 1 in. (2.5cm) chain, 2–4mm links
- **2** 2-in. (5cm) head pins
- pair of earring wires
- chainnose and roundnose pliers
- diagonal wire cutters

1 **pendant with jump ring bail** • To make the bail (the pendant's hanging loop): Open a 10mm jump ring (Basics, p. 12.) Attach another 10mm jump ring, and close the first jump ring. Attach a third 10mm jump ring to the first two jump rings.

2 On a 3-in. (7.6cm) head pin, string: small spacer, two gemstone chips, small spacer, focal bead, large spacer, two chips, large spacer. Make the first half of a wrapped loop (Basics). Attach the dangle to the jump ring bail. Complete the wraps.

1 **pendant with chain dangles** • **a** On a 3-in. (7.6cm) head pin, string a gemstone nugget, beads, and spacers as desired. Make the first half of a wrapped loop (Basics, p. 12). On four 2-in. (5cm) head pins, string beads and spacers as desired. Make the first half of a wrapped loop on each.

b To make chain dangles, cut five pieces of chain to the following lengths: two ⅜ in. (1cm), two ¾ in. (1.9cm), and one 1 in. (2.5cm). Attach the nugget's loop to a ⅜-in. (1cm) piece of chain. Attach each remaining bead unit to a chain. Complete the wraps.

2 Open a 10mm jump ring (Basics). Attach the chain dangles to a bail. Close the jump ring.

1 **necklace** • Determine the finished length of your necklace. (My necklaces are 19 in./48cm.) Subtract 8 in. (20cm) and cut a piece of leather cord to that length. Subtract 12 in. (30cm) from the finished length and cut three pieces of chain, each to that length.

Apply glue to each end of the leather cord and attach a crimp end. Using chainnose pliers, flatten the center portion of the crimp end.

2 Open a 6mm jump ring (Basics, p. 12). Attach the three pieces of chain and one of the crimp ends. Close the jump ring.

3 Open a 6mm jump ring. Attach the other ends of the chains and a lobster claw clasp. Close the jump ring.

1 **earrings** • On a 2-in. (5cm) head pin, string: 4mm crystal, 4mm spacer, gemstone chip, 6mm crystal, chip, spacer, 4mm crystal. Make the first half of a wrapped loop (Basics, p. 12). Cut a ⅜-in. (1cm) piece of chain. Attach the loop and complete the wraps.

2 Open the loop of an earring wire (Basics). Attach the dangle and close the loop. Make a second earring to match the first. ❖

DESIGN GUIDELINES
- The polymer clay bead attached to the jump ring bail was made by Emma Ralph, ejrbeads.co.uk.
- In the pendant with chain dangles, match a few of the crystals to the focal bead.

Weaving
a better life

Pair beaded beads with suede
for an organic look

by Cathy Jakicic

Nguni Imports' beads come from a variety of sources in the Republic of South Africa, but they're primarily made by the Zulu people of the Kwa-Zulu Natal Province. The Nguni women artisans hand weave the beads in their homes so they can also take care of their families. For many women, this is their sole source of income, providing money for basic needs and, for a few, school fees and supplies. For more information or to purchase beads or finished jewelry, visit nguni.com.

SUPPLY NOTE
Substitute silk cord for the suede for a dressier look.

1 necklace • a Determine the finished length of your necklace. (Mine is 37 in./.94m.) Add 1 in. (2.5cm) for each bead, and cut a piece of cord to that length.

b Center a bead on the cord. Tie an overhand knot (Basics, p. 12) on each side of the bead.

2 On each end, 2–3 in. (5–7.6cm) from the last knot, tie an overhand knot, string a bead, and tie an overhand knot. Repeat.

3 a On one end, 2–3 in. (5–7.6cm) from the last knot, tie an overhand knot, string a bead, and tie an overhand knot.

b On the other end, 2–3 in. (5–7.6cm) from the last knot, attach a felt ring with an overhand knot.

c On each end, repeat step 3a once or twice.

4 Check the fit, and trim cord from each end if necessary. On each end, apply adhesive to the cord. Attach a crimp end (Basics).

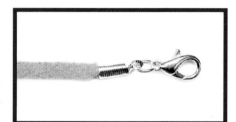

5 On one end, open a jump ring (Basics) and attach the crimp end's loop and a lobster claw clasp. Close the jump ring. Repeat on the other end, omitting the clasp.

1 earrings • Cut a 5-in. (13cm) piece of cord. Tie an overhand knot (Basics, p. 12) on one end. String a bead, and tie another overhand knot.

2 On one end, apply adhesive to the cord. Attach a crimp end (Basics). Open the loop of an earring wire (Basics) and attach the dangle. Close the loop. Make a second earring to match the first. ✤

A decorative dangle is anything but ordinary

Steeped in charm

by Steven James

Extract the most from your next teatime experience by adding beads to your tea infuser's chain. Brew for two? Add your favorite loose leaves and a mug for a comforting gift for a frazzled friend.

1 **infuser with briolette** •
Cut a 4-in. (10cm) piece
of 24-gauge wire. String a
briolette 1 in. (2.5cm) from one
end, and bend the wire upward
to form a U shape. Make a
wrapped loop (Basics, p. 12)
with the longer wire, extending
wraps down and around the
top of the briolette.

2 Cut an 8-in. (20cm) piece
of beading wire. String a
crimp bead and the briolette
unit. Go back through the
crimp bead, tighten the
wire, and crimp the crimp
bead (Basics).

3 String 3 in. (7.6cm) of
crystals, spacers, and 6º
seed beads.
    If the tea infuser has a
hook attached to its chain,
remove it.

4 String a crimp bead
and the chain. Go back
through the last few beads
strung, and tighten the wire.
Crimp the crimp bead and
trim the excess wire.

1 **infuser with charm** • Cut
a ½-in. (1.3cm) piece of
chain. Cut a 2-in. (5cm) piece
of 24-gauge wire. Make the
first half of a wrapped loop
on one end (Basics, p. 12).
Attach the chain and
complete the wraps. Make
three chain units.

2 String a crystal on one
wire and make the first
half of a wrapped loop.
Attach a chain unit and
complete the wraps. Repeat.

3 String a crystal on the wire
and make the first half of
a wrapped loop. Attach an
infuser's hook and complete
the wraps.

4 Open a jump ring (Basics).
Attach a charm and the
remaining chain end. Close
the jump ring. ❖

Suspend beads in a

To unify the different types of beads in this bracelet, choose crystals and gemstones to reflect the colors in the focal bead. Make big, bold hoop earrings to match.

A mix of dangles and beads looks whimsical

lush bracelet

by Joanna Mueller

1 bracelet • On a head pin, string beads and spacers as desired, and make the first half of a wrapped loop (Basics, p. 12). Make 25 to 40 dangles. Set one dangle aside for step 7.

2 Attach each dangle to a soldered jump ring and complete the wraps. On some jump rings, attach a second dangle.

3 To make a top-drilled-bead dangle: Cut a 3-in. (7.6cm) piece of wire. String the bead and make a set of wraps above it (Basics). Make the first half of a wrapped loop above the wraps. Attach a soldered jump ring and complete the wraps.

4 To make a charm dangle: Open a 4mm jump ring (Basics). Attach the charm and a soldered jump ring. Close the jump ring.

If desired, attach a second 4mm jump ring and a dangle.

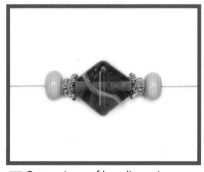

5 Cut a piece of beading wire (Basics). On the wire, center: 6–15mm bead, bead cap, focal bead, bead cap, 6–15mm bead.

6 On each end, string a dangle and a 6–15mm bead. Repeat until the bracelet is within 1 in. (2.5cm) of the desired length. End with a 6–15mm bead.

Make fun earrings to complete your look

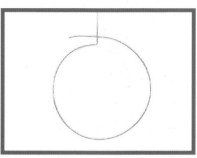

1 earrings • Cut an 8-in. (20cm) piece of wire. Wrap it around a round object with an approximately 2-in. (5cm) diameter.

Make a stem by bending ½ in. (1.3cm) of the wire up at a right angle.

2 String a crystal, five beads, and a crystal. Make a set of wraps (Basics, p. 12) around the stem. Make a plain loop (Basics).

3 Hammer the hoop on a bench block or anvil, being careful not to break the beads.

4 Open the loop of an earring wire (Basics). Attach the hoop and close the loop. Make a second earring to match the first. ❖

7 To make an extender: Cut a 1-in. (2.5cm) piece of chain. Attach a dangle to the chain. Complete the wraps.

8 On one end, string a spacer, a crimp bead, a spacer, and a lobster claw clasp. Repeat on the other end, substituting the extender for the clasp. Check the fit, and add or remove beads from each end if necessary. Go back through the beads just strung and tighten the wire. Crimp the crimp beads (Basics) and trim the excess wire.

Supply List

bracelet
- 15–25mm focal bead
- **60–80** 3–15mm beads (lampworked beads by Joanna Mueller, sleekbeads.com)
- **2–5** 15–20mm metal charms
- **20–30** 3–6mm spacers
- **2** bead caps for focal bead
- flexible beading wire, .018 or .019
- 24-gauge half-hard wire (3 in./7.6cm for each top-drilled bead)
- 1 in. (2.5cm) chain, 5–6mm links
- **25–40** 2-in. (5cm) head pins
- **20–30** 5mm soldered jump rings
- **2–10** 4mm jump rings
- **2** crimp beads
- lobster claw clasp
- chainnose and roundnose pliers
- diagonal wire cutters
- crimping pliers (optional)

earrings
- **10** 6–9mm beads
- **4** 4mm crystals
- 16 in. (41cm) 20-gauge half-hard wire
- pair of earring wires
- chainnose and roundnose pliers
- diagonal wire cutters
- ball-peen hammer
- bench block or anvil

Make it
YOUR
STYLE

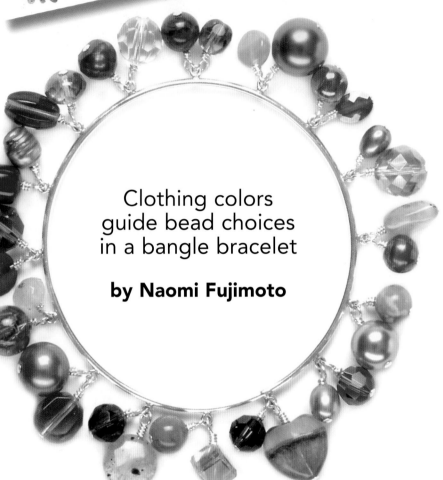

Clothing colors guide bead choices in a bangle bracelet

by Naomi Fujimoto

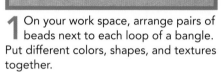

1 On your work space, arrange pairs of beads next to each loop of a bangle. Put different colors, shapes, and textures together.

2 On a head pin, string a bead. Make the first half of a wrapped loop (Basics, p. 12). Make 32 bead units.

3 Attach a pair of bead units to a loop of the bangle. Complete the wraps.

4 Attach the remaining pairs of bead units to the bangle loops. ❖

DESIGN OPTION

In my bracelet, I used pairs of beads. For a fuller bracelet, you can attach three or four beads to each bangle loop.

Supply List

- **32** 6–12mm beads
- 16-loop bangle bracelet (Auntie's Beads, 866-262-3237, auntiesbeads.com)
- **32** 1½-in. (3.8cm) head pins
- chainnose and roundnose pliers
- diagonal wire cutters

One strand, many styles

A necklace and bracelet are long on possibilities

by Andrea Loss

Quickly string this extra-long necklace, and you'll be changing styles with ease. Wrap it multiple times for a chic choker or twice for a princess-length necklace. Or, wear it casually as one long strand.

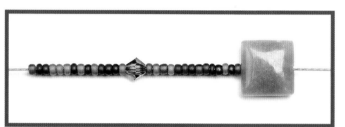

1 necklace • Cut a piece of beading wire (Basics, p. 12). (My necklace is 44 in./1.1m.) String 14 11º seed beads, a bicone crystal, 14 11ºs, and a square bead. Repeat until the necklace is within 2 in. (5cm) of the finished length. End with 11ºs.

2 On each end, string a crimp bead, an 11º, and half of a clasp. Check the fit, and add or remove beads from each end if necessary. Go back through the last few beads strung and tighten the wire. Crimp the crimp beads (Basics) and trim the excess wire.

bracelet • Cut a piece of beading wire (Basics, p. 12). String eight 11º seed beads, a bicone crystal, eight 11ºs, and a square bead. Repeat until the strand is within 2 in. (5cm) of the finished length. End with 11ºs. Finish as in step 2 of the necklace. ❖

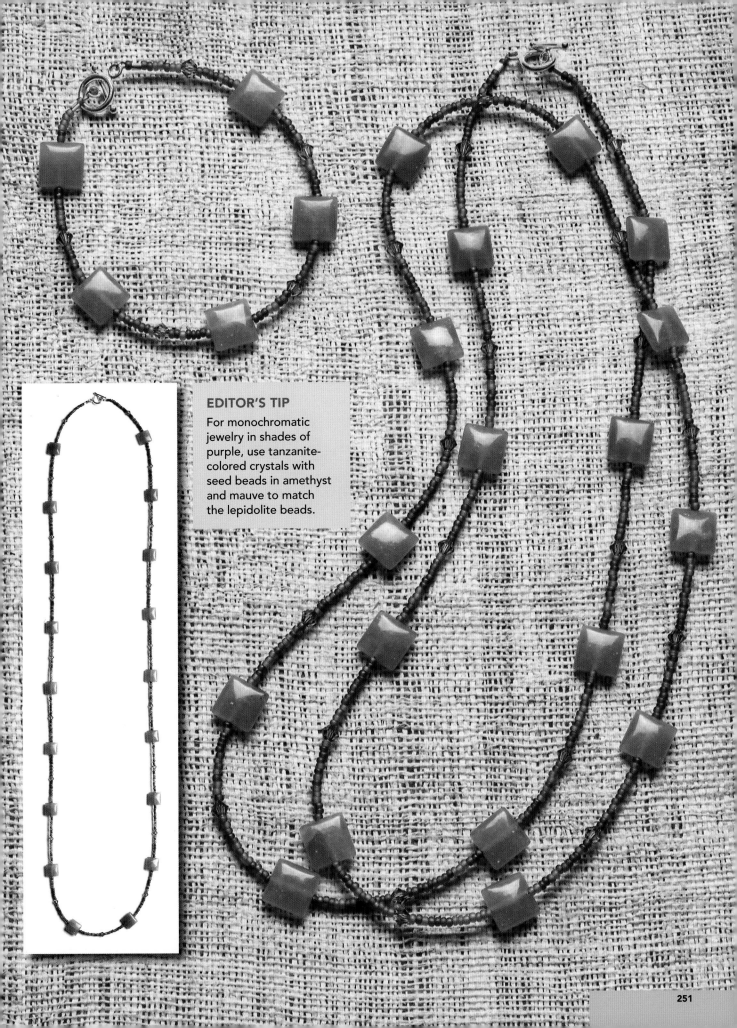

Add sparkle to a
timeless design

1 Cut a piece of beading wire (Basics, p. 12). Center four pearls on the wire, positioning the pearls in opposite directions.

2 On each end, string a polygon-drop crystal and four pearls. Repeat until the strand is within 2 in. (5cm) of the desired length.

3 On each end, string a bicone crystal, a crimp bead, a bicone, and half of the clasp. Check the fit, and add or remove beads from each end if necessary. Go back through the beads just strung and tighten the wire. Crimp the crimp bead (Basics) and trim the excess wire. ✿

Update a
by **Irina Miech**
pearl bracelet

For a fresh version of the classic pearl bracelet, mingle top-drilled pearls with the most up-to-date crystal shape.

EDITOR'S TIPS
- Because polygon-drop crystals are available in limited colors (see a few at right), choose those first, and then select pearls to coordinate.
- For color with dimension, use a strand of multicolored pearls.

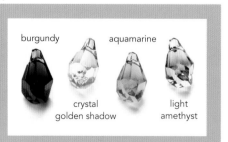

burgundy   aquamarine

crystal
golden shadow   light
amethyst

Supply List

- **5–7** 13mm polygon-drop crystals (Eclectica, 262-641-0910)
- **22–28** 8–12mm pearls, top drilled
- **4** 4mm bicone crystals
- flexible beading wire, .014 or .015
- **2** crimp beads
- toggle clasp
- chainnose or crimping pliers
- diagonal wire cutters

Shortcuts

Readers' tips to make your beading life easier

1 bead caddy

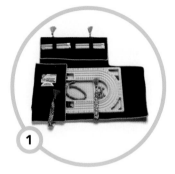

I made a bead caddy and work mat that I can roll up mid-project when I need to. The work surface is large enough for a beading board, the side flaps have pockets to store supplies, and the loops on the outside hold tools or other items.
– *Laura Daily, Carmel, Ind.*

4 heishi help

Heishi beads can be difficult to pick up and string. Stringing size .018 (or narrower) flexible beading wire through the beads while they are still on their original thread saves time when adding heishis to a strand. This method also works well with sequins.
– *Debbie Tuttle, Ballston Lake, N.Y.*

2 easy elastic stringing

To string beads more easily on ribbon elastic, fold a 2–3-in. (5–7.6cm) piece of flexible beading wire and simply string beads over both ends of the wire. Transfer the beads from the wire onto the elastic.
– *Luann Cowdrey, Tulsa, Okla.*

5 mobile earring display

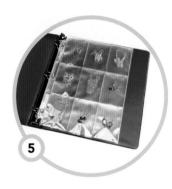

Sports-card pages are a convenient way to transport and display earrings for sale. Close the top of the packets with double-stick tape to keep the earrings secure while still allowing buyers to remove them for a closer look.
– *Nicole Jeske, Minocqua, Wis.*

3 bead scoop

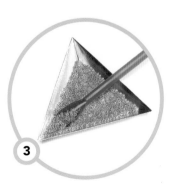

Slushee straws are perfect for scooping up small beads. Pick up beads with the spoon end and empty them into a storage container through the straw end.
– *Cheryl Finley, Oak Park, Ill.*

Contributors

Lori Anderson, a full-time jewelry artist, works in Easton, Md. Contact her at lori@lorianderson.net or via lorianderson.net.

Rupa Balachandar is passionate about gems and jewelry and contributes regularly to *BeadStyle* magazine. Visit her Web site, rupab.com or e-mail her at info@rupab.com.

Arleen Bejerano designs jewelry and teaches beading classes at Chic Beads in Los Alamitos, Calif. Contact her at arbejerano@hotmail.com.

Contact **Lisa Belden** via her Web site at cuttlefishjewelry.com.

Paulette Biedenbender owns Bead Needs in Hales Corners, Wis. Reach her at (414) 529-5211, or visit her Web site, beadneedsllc.com.

Contact **Teri Bienvenue** in care of *BeadStyle*.

Contact **Karen Burdette** at kburdette@kalmbach.com.

Christianne and Maria Camera co-own Bella Bella! in Milwaukee, Wis. Contact them in care of *BeadStyle* magazine.

Jenna Colyar-Cooper, a life-long beader, currently works for fusionbeads.com. Contact Jenna at jenna@fusionbeads.com.

Contact **Gloria Farver** via e-mail at rfarver@wi.rr.com.

Naomi Fujimoto, *BeadStyle* Senior Editor, is the author of *Cool Jewels: Beading Projects for Teens*. Contact her in care of *BeadStyle*.

Contact **Jeanne Gassert** in care of Kalmbach Books.

Sue Godfrey's jewelry designs are in several boutiques in Wisconsin. Contact her at highstrungsue@wi.rr.com.

Contact **Mia Gofar** via e-mail at mia@miagofar.com or the Web site miagofar.com.

Marla Gulotta's passion is designing new jewelry with an eye to the past. Reach her at attolug@sbcglobal.net.

Monica Han is an award-winning mixed-media jewelry designer and teacher in Potomac, Md. Contact her at mhan@dreambeads.biz.

Contact **Linda Hartung** via e-mail at linda@alacarteclasps.com or through her Web sites, alacarteclasps.com or wirelace.com.

Lindsay Hastings works and teaches in Loveland, Ohio. Contact her via e-mail at phoenixrisingdesigns@yahoo.com or her Web site, freewebs.com/phoenixrisingdesigns.

Contact **Heidi Hermreck** in care of Pam Israel at Via Murano, pam@viamurano.com, or visit viamurano.com.

Contact **Deb Huber** at dlhuber@comcast.net or the Web site clever-treasures.com.

Cathy Jakicic is Editor of *BeadStyle*. Contact her through the magazine.

"What are you gonna make today?," asks **Steven James**, who incorporates beads and jewelry-making into décor and everyday living. Visit his Web site, macaroniandglitter.com.

Contact **Devona J. Jefferson** via e-mail at info@chicadornments.com or her Web site at chicadornments.etsy.com.

Contact **Eva Kapitany** in care of *BeadStyle*.

Contact **Lanie Ketcherside** in care of Kalmbach Books.

Contact **Trish Kirkham** via e-mail at miayadesigns@hotmail.com or her Web site at kirkhamstudios.com.

Teresa Kodatt makes beads and jewelry, and teaches at her store, Pumpkin Glass, in Morton, Ill. Contact her at teresa@pumpkinglass.com or visit pumpkinglass.com.

Jane Konkel, Associate Editor at *BeadStyle*, indulges her crafty side as a contributor to *Make it Mine*. Contact her in care of *BeadStyle*.

Deborah Lacher is a full-time nurse in Ohio, but her love is making jewelry. Contact Deborah via e-mail at debbe2000@yahoo.com.

Contact **Andrea Loss** via e-mail at amloss@wi.rr.com.

Jewelry designer **Monica Lueder** can be reached at mdesign@wi.rr.com.

Contact **Carol McKinney** at carolsjewelryandgifts@yahoo.com or through her Web site, carolsjewelryandgifts.com.

Irina Miech owns Eclectica in Brookfield, Wis. She is the author of the three metal clay jewelry books, as well as many beading and design articles. Contact her via e-mail at eclecticainfo@sbcglobal.net, or visit eclecticabeads.com.

Contact **Roxie Moede** at rmoede@kalmbach.com.

Contact **Joanna Mueller** at sleekbeads@yahoo.com or her Web site at sleekbeads.com.

Contact **Linda Osterhoudt** via e-mail at lindaoohlinda@earthlink.net or the Web site ohlinda.com.

Between raising monarch butterflies and teaching beading classes in northern Wis., **Julie Paasch-Anderson** of Milwaukee enjoys creating unique and versatile jewelry. Contact her via e-mail at jpadesigns@ameritech.net.

Polymer-clay bead artist **Heather Powers** is the creative force behind Bead Cruise, Bead Week, and the Art Bead Scene. Visit her web site, humblebeads.com.

Tammy Powley is a jewelry designer and author of various books, blogs, and a Web site. For more information, visit tammypowley.com, or e-mail tammypowley@yahoo.com.

Contact **Paloma Ramos-Tapia** via e-mail at blkndvudu@mac.com or view her work online at rubylane.com/shops/moonlitbayou.

Reach **Robyn Rosen** via e-mail at robyn@robynrosen.com or visit robynrosen.com.

Brenda Schweder, a frequent contributor to Kalmbach titles, is author of the book *Junk to Jewelry*. See more at her Web site, brendaschweder.com, or contact her at b@brendaschweder.com.

Kathie Scrimgeour has been published in *BeadStyle* and online in the *Bead Bugle*. Contact her at kjscrim@yahoo.com.

Contact **Debbi Simon** at dsimon@kalmbach.com.

Contact **Ann Smith** at asmith@kalmbach.com.

Sara Strauss was trained in jewelry design at the Fashion Institute of Technology in New York. Contact her via e-mail at bluestaro@hotmail.com or visit her Web site, sgsjewelry.com.

Karli Sullivan co-owns Confetti: The Bead Place, in Surprise, Ariz. Contact her at (623) 975-7250, via e-mail at madredolce@yahoo.com or on her Web site, confettibeads.com.

Helene Tsigistras' jewelry has been featured in *BeadStyle* and *Bead&Button*, as well as in several books. Contact her via e-mail at htsigistras@kalmbach.com.

Contact **Deborah Tuttle** via her Web site at bijouxcreations.com.

Wendy Witchner is a wire and metal jewelry artist who constantly travels the United States in her motor home to sell her creations at art shows. Her work also is available at select galleries. Visit her Web site, wendywitchner-jewelry.com.

Cynthia B. Wuller is a Chicago-based artist who loves jewelry design, fiber arts, and painting. She is the author of *Inspired Wire*. Contact her at cbwuller@yahoo.com.

Jean Yates of Westchester County, N.Y., creates beading tutorials and has recently written a jewelry design book titled *Links*. For more, see prettykittydogmoonjewelry.com, or visit her blog at prettykittydogmoonjewelry.blogspot.com.